Collected for Mercedes-Benz
from the Country Garden Cookbook Series.

Picnics

OVER 40 RECIPES FOR DINING IN THE GREAT OUTDOORS
FROM MERCEDES-BENZ.

Edited with Introduction by Heidi Haughy Cusick

Photography by Deborah Jones and Kathryn Kleinman
Featuring recipes from the Country Garden Cookbook *series:*
Apples *by Christopher Idone* • Berries *by Sharon Kramis*
Greens *by Sibella Kraus* • Lemons *by Christopher Idone*
Potatoes *by Maggie Waldron* • Tomatoes *by Jesse Ziff Cool*

CollinsPublishersSanFrancisco
A Division of HarperCollins*Publishers*

Mercedes-Benz

First published in USA 1994 by Collins Publishers San Francisco
Copyright © 1994 Collins Publishers San Francisco
See additional copyright information on page 94.
HarperCollins Web Site: http://www.harpercollins.com
HarperCollins®, 🏭 ® and CollinsPublishersSanFrancisco™
are trademarks of HarperCollins Publishers Inc.
Creative Director: Jennifer Barry
Designer: Kari Perin
Series Editor: Meesha Halm
The napkin illustration on page 37 is from The Best of the Old Farmer's Almanac
by Will Forpe. Copyright © 1977 by Jonathan David Publishers.
Reprinted with the permission of Jonathan David Publishers.

Library of Congress Cataloging-in-Publication Data
Picnics: over 40 recipes for dining in the great outdoors collected from the country garden
cookbook series / edited with introduction by Heidi Haughy Cusick;
photography by Deborah Jones and Kathryn Kleinman.
p.   cm.
Includes index.
ISBN 0-06-019324-7
1. Outdoor cookery.   2. Picnicking.   I. Cusick, Heidi Haughy.
TX823.P527 1994
641.5'78 – dc20   CIP 94-21598
Printed in China
1 3 5 7 9 10 8 6 4 2

Acknowledgments
Collins Publishers would like to thank all the
Country Garden Cookbook authors and photographers;
Sandra Cook and Stephanie Greenleigh, food stylists;
Michaele Thunen and Sara Slavin, floral and prop stylists;
and Kristen Wurz, design and production coordinator.

CONTENTS

INTRODUCTION

Going on picnics is like falling in love. Serene, delicious, wholesome, intimate, unpredictable. A blanket spread on the forest floor or a grassy hillside prompts an anticipation of adventure. He reaches across the basket to touch your hand. The kids run off to catch a butterfly. A friend grabs a Frisbee and another uncorks the wine. The air is fresh and the appetite is stimulated. Expectations mount as the basket is unpacked.

Picnics reflect levels of know-how, adaptability and adventurousness, as well as intimacy, infatuation and maturity. By their nature, they require at least two people. A solo jaunt, even with a tidy basket of food in hand, is too personal to address here. Besides, the meaning of picnic is from the French phrase *pique-nique,* referring to a meal eaten outdoors for which each participant brings a dish. Enticing you into sharing your blanket with others and preparing a thoughtful repast is my goal.

Like love, picnics appeal to all the senses. Fresh air clarifies vision for studying a wild mushroom. Smoldering coals emanate smoky vapors. An autumn breeze brushes across your skin. A chorus of songbirds fills the air. And then you eat, as if it's the first time.

While dining outside appeals to our primal side, it can also be a challenge. On one hand, a picnic is like a minivacation because it takes us away from the usual routine. Site possibilities are limited only by personal preferences, imagination and time. We can go hiking or skiing and eat trailside; carry a lunch to the pool or the beach; or fire up the barbecue at a city park or state campground. At the same time, rain, wind and cold test the abilities of even the most avid picnickers. A tarp tied to the trees can help, but requires resourcefulness and ingenuity. Insects often come with the territory, as do thieving blue jays and the occasional bold squirrel. But the thrill of having defied the elements can lead to the most memorable meal ever.

The most relaxing picnics are those that have been thought out in advance. Even if spontaneous, the best experience comes from the old scouting motto: Be Prepared. In the Picnicking Logistics section is a list of equipment and staples to keep on hand. That way,

whether you are planning a celebratory picnic for dozens or you suddenly decide to head to the park for dinner with your family after work, the napkins, plates, utensils and matches are packed and ready to go. This section also offers practical counsels and cautions regarding food storage. And I share a method for preparing the barbecue fire that avoids using chemical-laced briquettes and lighter fuels.

What precipitates a picnic depends on you. A new park opens. The love of your life needs a break. You haven't seen your friends in ages. The weather is balmy and evenings are light and warm. The autumn leaves are changing color. The spring wildflowers are blooming. You are hungry.

We already know everything tastes better outdoors. Salt, sweet, bitter and tart gain an intensity in the open air that is only hinted at when trapped indoors. Tuna between two pieces of bread or atop a nicoise salad tastes sea-fresh and slightly salty when eaten while sitting on a redwood bench or on the beach.

Because of their informality, picnics are a wonderful way to entertain. In the Special Occasion Menus section are suggestions for six theme picnics, for which either the host

prepares everything or everyone participates by bringing a special dish. In addition to the recipes are ideas for locations and accoutrements to embellish and complement the themes. Guests can also be asked to contribute a story, game or table decoration. Themes range from a romantic picnic for two to an Independence Day celebration for twenty.

I grew up going on picnics. On Sunday outings in the car, my mom always packed a lunch, partly for the economics of feeding seven children, and mostly because destinations were usually parks. My husband courted me with picnics shared on coastal headlands, Sierra mountain peaks and Provençal hillsides. Now,

my children, who often ate packed lunches on benches and blankets, raid the refrigerator for olives and cheese to take on their own backpacking excursions in the redwoods or canoeing trips up the river.

Every day presents an occasion for picnicking; from Sunday breakfast and Saturday lunch to a sunset dinner. Every recipe here deserves an occasion. Soon, you'll be lazing on a blanket, edibles at your fingertips, with the only sounds around you those you don't have to answer. In addition to being serene, delicious, wholesome, intimate and unpredictable, picnics are also rejuvenating and satisfying—just like falling in love.

PICNICKING LOGISTICS

To ensure a successful picnic, whether a spur-of-the-moment or a set occasion, some planning and cautionary details are important. Any of the recipes in this book are suitable for car-carried picnics. Except when directed to pack in a cooler until ready to serve, many of the recipes can also be tucked into backpacks for day hikes.

Equipment: First, you need something to carry the food in. A grocery bag or a cardboard box will do. But a basket—whether an antique woven one with a solid wood lid, a big, open-topped wicker affair or an elaborate china-and-flatware-stocked hamper—is preferable. Line it with a square of gingham or chintz, and the aesthetic appeal of the picnic basket is matched only by its Pandora's box potential.

I keep a basket stocked with the essentials. Everything is as lightweight as possible, since our picnics are usually carted a fair hike from the house or the car to the site. I recommend stocking the hamper with reusable place settings and utensils whenever possible. This means you'll have to do the dishes when you return, but it makes good environmental sense.

Here's what I recommend keeping on hand:

Plastic plates or wide, shallow bowls that double as plates
Stack of paper plates (optional)
Reusable heavy-duty plastic forks, knives and spoons
Reusable heavy-duty plastic glasses
Paper or lightweight cloth napkins
Paper towels
Matches
Corkscrew
Bread knife
Small cutting board
Tablecloth that doubles as a basket liner
Picnic blanket
Thermos
Thermal-insulated containers

In addition, an assortment of plastic bowls or rectangular containers with tight-fitting lids is indispensable. A plastic cake carrier is also a great invention. To keep pies and tarts fresh looking, invert aluminum pie tins over the top and secure them with rubber bands or string.

You need a cooler and a bag of ice or packets of frozen blue ice for transporting salads and dairy products and for keeping drinks cold. A thermos is perfect for soups, coffee and other hot or cold drinks.

A portable folding grill is ideal for cooking over open fires at a beach or campsite. Keep it wrapped in newspaper and rewrap it when it has cooled before taking it home.

For theme picnics I like to pack accessories to set the mood. Sometimes I take a special serving plate, vase or pitcher. Choose printed fabrics, from English-garden chintz to patriotic prints, to use as tablecloths and napkins.

Cautions: The appeal of picnics is to dine outdoors. Since most picnics are enjoyed at midday, when the sun is the hottest, a few precautionary measures must be taken to prevent food from spoiling. Clearly, potato chips left in the sun don't take long to become stale and tasteless. They probably won't hurt you, but mayonnaise that gets too hot can become toxic. Always use commercial mayonnaise on a picnic. The preservatives do prolong—although they don't prevent— its heat resistance. Cheese, butter and other dairy products will also spoil if they get too hot. Fully chill any dishes containing butter or cheese in the refrigerator before

packing them in a cooler. Leave them in the cooler until serving time. Instructions for chilling and packing are included with each recipe.

To keep lettuce and other vegetables and fruits fresh, wash, dry and pack in plastic bags or reusable plastic containers. Chill them in the refrigerator for at least a couple of hours before taking them to the picnic, preferably in a cooler.

To minimize the attraction of insects and flies, store food on a table, shielded with a fine mesh screen or other covering, or in covered containers until ready to serve. Bees are attracted to meats and sweets. The old advice not to make them angry still holds true. Ignoring them won't necessarily make them go away, but it should prevent them from stinging. Insect sprays and first-aid kits are good to take along if you are going somewhere where such infestations are possible.

Barbecue: Since picnics and barbecues go together naturally, you'll want to prepare the best coals possible for grilling. Whenever I make a fire at the beach, I remember the time my college roommates and I used poison oak as kindling. By the next day, most of us had swollen, itchy welts everywhere, and one of us was in the hospital with poison oak in his esophagus! If you are going to a beach or park, make sure that the wood is safe and that collecting it is allowed. Otherwise, bring your own kindling and logs.

Build the fire in a contained space with plenty of sand around it or in a barbecue pit. This is how to do it. You will need:

Newspaper

Kindling

Several split hardwood logs, such as oak, madrone,
   alder or hickory or

Hunks of hardwood charcoal, such as mesquite

Cooking oil

Matches

Oak, alder, hickory or fruitwood chips (optional)

Portable grill rack (if not provided at the location)

Basting brush

Start with crumpled newspaper. Pile it on the bottom of the pit. Top it with kindling and then the split wood or hardwood coals. Sprinkle a little cooking oil over the top and light the paper. If necessary, stoke the fire from below to get oxygen to the flames and to keep it burning as furiously as possible so the large wood starts smoldering. Once lit, the fire will take 20 to 30 minutes, depending on the size of the pile, to reduce to grill-perfect heat. When the fire has burned to the coal stage, spread out the coals and place the grill rack over them to heat it well before adding the food. Brush a little oil on the rack just before cooking. If using wood chips, soak them in water for 20 minutes and add during cooking to impart a smoky flavor to the food. Alder goes especially well with salmon, hickory is a natural with pork and fruitwood complements chicken.

When grilling herb-marinated foods, tie a bunch of the fresh herbs together to make a basting brush, as is suggested in the recipe for Rosemary Potato Skewers. When grilling bread, as in Caponata on Bruschetta, place the bread slices on the hot grill next to, but not over, the coals to keep from burning them.

If you need to melt cheese, such as in Marinated Cherry Tomatoes over Warm Provolone Garlic Bread, take along an old pot lid or make a tent with a piece of aluminum foil to reflect the heat to the top.

Final Note: Don't forget to take all your garbage with you when you leave, and most importantly, have a great time.

SPECIAL OCCASION MENUS

Spring Breakfast

Serves 4 to 6

A batch of scones, a jug of coffee and dawn. Rise early to watch the day begin from a beautiful hillside carpeted with wildflowers or in a park surrounded by the ringing chorus of a hundred mating birds. Make everything but the coffee and smoothies the day before. Double the recipes for the smoothies and the compote. You'll have more scones and muffins than you need, so freeze or store them in the refrigerator for the next day. The orange scones can also be served without the berries and cream. Just before setting out, brew the coffee and blend the smoothies, and then leave the morning newspaper at home.

Frittata with Chard and Roasted Red Peppers
Strawberry Grapefruit Mint Compote
Blueberry Banana Muffins
Prizewinning Orange Scones with Berries and Cream
Bloody Mary
Strawberry Pineapple Smoothie
Freshly Brewed Coffee

Dejeuner sur l'Herbe

Serves 4

Romantic visions of picnics created by Monet, Manet and Cézanne in their interpretations of *le dejeuner sur l'herbe,* and by our own fantasies, suggest a blanket on the lawn, wide-brimmed hats, flowers in bloom, billowy clouds and a concerto of songbirds. If the day is balmy enough, you may even choose to wear as little as the nude in Manet's famous painting. Choose a park, estate or forest setting for this lovely menu and serve everything on the blanket. Don't forget the parasol.

Open-Faced Watercress Sandwiches
Prosciutto Stuffed with Red Chard
Baby Artichoke Salad
Country French Potato Salad
Salad of Herbs
Black, Golden and Red Raspberry Tart
Blackberry Spritzer
French Beaujolais or California Pinot Noir

Autumn Courtship in an Italian Garden

Serves 2

In the warmth of early autumn, before the leaves turn, a light breeze briefly chills the air with season-changing significance. With the crowds gone, your favorite public garden is a serene setting for a picnic for two. Invite your heart-throb and serve this Italian-inspired fare on a red-checkered tablecloth set with china plates and crystal wineglasses. To prepare everything ahead, lightly toast baguette slices and make little open-faced sandwiches with one or more of the sandwich recipes. Make a half recipe of both the Salmagundi and the arugula sandwiches. Pack the olives you made a month earlier and as many lemon squares as you think you'll both eat. Don't forget a bouquet for the table . . . and a collection of Italian love sonnets.

Salmagundi
Arugula, Roasted Red Peppers and Prosciutto
  on Panini
Olives Spiced with Lemon and Herbs
Lemon Squares
Chianti Classico

Trailside Winter Picnic

Serves 4

Everything on this menu can go into the back-pack for a cross-country ski sojourn or a New Year's Day hike in the woods. Substitute left-over turkey for the roasted chicken and pack it for a rejuvenating hike the day after Thanks-giving. And if the weather becomes relentless, eat these spicy, savory and sweet flavors in front of your living room fireplace. For four people, use two carrots and one medium jicama for the chili-spiced recipe and take as much of the apple crisp as you think you will eat.

Chili-Spiced Jicama and Carrots
Roasted Chicken and Watercress Sandwiches
  with Cranberry Orange Apple Relish
Apple and Dried Cranberry Crisp
Hot Rum and Cider

Dionysus' Feast

Serves 8

Dionysus was the Greek god of wine and fertility who loved to have a good time. Plan this Mediterranean barbecue in his honor for sunset on a hot night. Inhale the oregano and rosemary aromas from the grilled sea bass and potatoes and imagine them drifting from heat-parched Greek hillsides. Let the feta from mountain-clinging sheep, the briny olives, zesty lemon and fruity olive oil found in Athenian markets play on your palate. Double all the recipes except the dessert. Cut the sandwiches into bite-sized appetizers. And watch the sun set over a vineyard, a lake or the sea.

Rosemary Potato Skewers
Dolmas Made with Chard Leaves
Caponata on Bruschetta
Bulgur Wheat and Parsley Salad
Squid Salad
Grilled Eggplant, Tomatoes, Provolone
* and Pesto Sandwiches*
Greek Islands Sea Bass
Tomato Ginger Upside-Down Cake
California Sauvignon Blanc or Italian Pinot Grigio

All-American Independence Day Barbecue

Serves 20

Hang up the bunting, invite the neighbors and light the barbecue. This Yankee Doodle menu highlights many of the foods America gave the world. It's a fitting way to celebrate our heritage. Buy a twelve- to fifteen-pound salmon and fillet it, leaving the whole fillets intact. Triple the recipes for the cucumber salsa, the potato and butter lettuce salads and the polenta. Make two crunches, at least four recipes of lemonade and a couple of batches of Lemon Shandies in memory of the British.

Watercress and Redleaf Lettuces with Orange,
* Red Onions and Fennel*
Red, White and Blue Potato Salad
Barbecued Salmon with Strawberry, Mint,
* and Cucumber Salsa*
Grilled Polenta with Sun-Dried Tomato Pesto
Corn on the Cob
Bray's Lemonade
Lemon Shandy
American Apple Pie
Marionberry Peach Crunch

SALADS & SIDES

A salad can be the satisfying centerpiece or a distinctive accompaniment to almost any picnic. Set one hearty Salmagundi or Salade Niçoise in the center of the blanket and everyone will happily nibble at its various ingredients for hours. Offer a salad of Chili-Spiced Jicama and Carrots or bring along Zucchini Marinated with Lemon and Mint to serve alongside grilled foods or sandwiches to lighten the menu.

In this chapter, you'll find a range of greens and other dressed ingredients to suit any picnic. Always pack the greens separately from the dressing until just ready to serve. When some of the salad ingredients are marinated in the dressing, such as in Fava Beans with Sun-Dried Tomato Oil and Pancetta on Frisée, pack them in their own container and scoop them onto the greens at the last minute.

Salade Niçoise

For an exceptional treat, prepare this wonderful version of Nice's best-known salad with poached or barbecued albacore. Otherwise, choose a good-quality canned tuna.

Approximately 2 pounds potatoes (6 medium), unpeeled, sliced 1/4 inch thick
Salt, to taste

Niçoise Dressing:
3/4 cup olive oil
6 tablespoons white wine vinegar
3 tablespoons water
3 tablespoons chopped fresh parsley
1 1/2 tablespoons drained capers
1 1/2 teaspoons dry mustard
1 large clove garlic, minced
1 1/2 teaspoons chopped fresh basil or 1/2 teaspoon dried basil

Lettuce leaves
3/4 pound assorted fresh vegetables (asparagus tips, trimmed green beans, snow peas, broccoli florets), cooked until crisp-tender
2 medium-sized ripe tomatoes, sliced
1 cup sliced mushrooms
1 bunch radishes, trimmed
2 cans (6 1/2 or 6 3/4 ounces each) water-packed tuna, drained and flaked, or 3/4 pound fresh albacore, poached or barbecued and sliced
Sprigs of fresh parsley, for garnish

In a heavy saucepan with a tight-fitting lid, place the potatoes. Add water to cover by 2 inches and salt to taste, cover and bring to a boil. Boil for approximately 8 minutes, or until tender when pierced. Drain and place in a large bowl.

Meanwhile, make the Niçoise Dressing. In a small bowl, whisk together the olive oil, vinegar, water, parsley, capers, mustard, garlic and basil.

Add half of the dressing to the still-warm potatoes and toss well. Cover and chill for at least 1 hour or for up to overnight. Place the remaining dressing in a leakproof container, cover tightly and refrigerate.

On a heavy portable plate, make a bed of lettuce leaves. Arrange the marinated potatoes, cooked vegetables, tomatoes, mushrooms, radishes and tuna over the lettuce leaves. Garnish with parsley. Cover with plastic wrap and pack for the picnic in a basket. Take along the remaining dressing to drizzle over the salad just before serving. *Serves 6*

Salmagundi

*One of the earliest examples of the composed salad, Salmagundi dates its
origins back to sixteenth-century England. Pack it, along with a crusty loaf of French bread,
and imagine yourself on a picnic outing on the manor grounds.*

Lemon Vinaigrette:
1/4 cup fresh lemon juice
Salt and freshly ground black pepper, to taste
1/3 cup walnut oil
2 tablespoons canola or vegetable oil

1/4 cup applejack (apple brandy)
1/4 cup water
1/2 cup golden raisins
1 small head looseleaf lettuce, washed and dried
2 heads Bibb lettuce, washed and dried
*3/4 pound haricots verts or green beans,
    cooked crisp-tender and drained*

1 cup pearl onions, blanched 3 minutes and peeled
*2 tart apples (such as Winesap or Granny Smith),
    peeled, quartered, cored and cut into
    1/4-inch dice*
1 cup seedless green grapes
1 tablespoon capers, drained
*6 boneless chicken breasts, poached and
    cut into long, thin strips*
*1/2 sweet red bell pepper, seeded, deribbed and
    cut into 1/4-inch dice*
6 quail eggs, hard-boiled, peeled and halved
1 tablespoon chopped fresh chives

To make the vinaigrette, in a small bowl, whisk together the lemon juice, salt and pepper. Gradually whisk in the oils until well blended. Set aside.

In a saucepan, combine the applejack and water. Bring to a simmer, add the raisins and set aside to cool.

Tear lettuce into bite-sized pieces, pack in a portable container and chill. Pack in the cooler for transporting.

In a large portable bowl with a lid, toss together the haricots verts, onions, apples, grapes,

and capers with enough of the vinaigrette to coat lightly. Place remaining vinaigrette in a container with a tight lid and pack in the cooler.

Drain the raisins and sprinkle over the salad. Arrange the chicken strips over the salad and sprinkle with the bell pepper. Place the quail eggs over the top and sprinkle with the chives. Cover and pack in the cooler. When ready to serve, place lettuce leaves on each plate and top with the salad. Drizzle with reserved vinaigrette.
Serves 6

Red, White and Blue Potato Salad

*If barbecued salmon is at the center of your grill
for Fourth of July picnics, leave the smoked salmon
out of this salad. If it's not on the grill, leave the
salmon in and serve the salad as a main dish.*

*Approximately 1 1/2 pounds assorted red, White
Rose and Peruvian Blue potatoes (4 or 5
medium), unpeeled, cut into 3/4-inch cubes*
Salt, to taste
5 tablespoons olive oil
3 tablespoons white wine vinegar
2 cloves garlic, minced
Salt and freshly ground black pepper, to taste
*6 ounces smoked salmon, cut into 1-inch-long strips
(optional)*
1/3 cup roughly chopped fresh chives
1/4 cup capers, drained
Fresh whole chives and paprika, for garnish

In a heavy saucepan with a tight-fitting lid, place
the potatoes. Add water to cover by 2 inches
and salt to taste, cover and bring to a boil. Boil for
approximately 15 minutes, or until tender when
pierced. Drain and let cool.

Meanwhile, in a large portable bowl, whisk
together the oil, vinegar and garlic. Season with
salt and pepper. Add the potatoes, salmon (if
using), chopped chives and capers and toss
gently. Garnish with whole chives and paprika.
Cover securely and pack in a picnic basket.
Serves 4 to 6

Country French Potato Salad

*The refreshing surprise of a minty dressing
is perfect after a strenuous hike or a vigorous swim.*

*1 1/2 pounds potatoes (4 medium), unpeeled, sliced
1/3 inch thick*
Salt, to taste

Garden Mint Dressing:
3/4 cup vegetable oil
4 to 6 tablespoons cider vinegar
2 tablespoons water
1 1/2 teaspoons dry mustard
1 teaspoon honey
1/4 cup minced green onions
3 tablespoons chopped fresh mint
Salt, to taste

*2 cups shelled fresh peas, cooked, or 1 package
(10 ounces) frozen peas, thawed*
*4 chicken breast halves, boned, skinned, poached,
drained and cooled*
Radishes and sprigs of fresh mint, for garnish

In a heavy saucepan with a tight-fitting lid, place
the potatoes. Add water to cover by 2 inches
and salt to taste, cover and bring to a boil. Boil
for approximately 8 minutes, or until tender
when pierced. Drain and let cool to lukewarm.

To make the dressing, in a small bowl,
whisk together the vegetable oil, vinegar, water,
mustard and honey. Stir in the green onions,
mint and salt.

In a large portable bowl, toss the potatoes and the peas with half of the dressing. In another portable bowl, toss the chicken with a few tablespoons of the dressing. Cover and refrigerate both bowls until they are packed for the picnic in the cooler. Put the radishes, mint sprigs and remaining dressing in small portable containers and pack in the cooler for transporting.

Just before serving, drizzle the remaining dressing over the potatoes. Cut each chicken breast crosswise into slices 1/3 inch.thick and arrange on top of the potatoes. Drizzle with any dressing remaining in the chicken container. Garnish with the radishes and mint. *Serves 4*

*Clockwise from bottom: Squid Salad, Bulgur Wheat and Parsley Salad,
Chili-Spiced Jicama and Carrots (recipe p. 25), Baby Artichoke Salad (recipe p. 26)
and Zucchini Marinated with Lemon and Mint (recipe p. 24)*

Bulgur Wheat and Parsley Salad

Mint and lemon complement the chewy texture of bulgur in this Middle Eastern classic. It can be a main dish or a side, whether camel riding in the desert, backpacking in the mountains or lounging on the lawn.

1/2 cup bulgur wheat (cracked wheat)
Boiling water, to cover
4 cups finely chopped fresh parsley
1 large red onion, finely chopped
3 large tomatoes, peeled, seeded and diced
1/2 cup finely chopped fresh mint
1 tablespoon grated lemon zest
Juice of 2 lemons
1/2 cup olive oil
Salt, to taste

Place the bulgur wheat in a large bowl and add enough boiling water to cover by about 1 inch. Set aside for 30 minutes.

In a large portable bowl, combine the parsley, onion, tomatoes, and mint. Set aside.

Drain the bulgur in a fine-mesh sieve, pressing down on the bulgur to extract the water. Turn out the bulgur onto a dry kitchen towel, wrap it in the towel and squeeze it dry. Place in a bowl and fluff with a fork to separate the grains. Then add the bulgur to the herb-tomato mixture, along with the lemon zest and juice. Stir gently. Drizzle the oil over the salad and toss to combine. Season with salt and toss again. Cover and refrigerate until chilled, and then pack in a picnic basket. *Serves 6*

Squid Salad

Its utter simplicity makes this salad a perfect partner to your more elaborate picnic fare. Fast cooking is the secret to keeping the shellfish tender. Tote crusty bread along for dipping into the tasty dressing.

2 pounds cleaned small squid
3/4 cup extra virgin olive oil
Kosher or coarse salt, to taste
Juice of 1 lemon
1/2 cup chopped fresh Italian parsley
1/4 teaspoon red pepper flakes, or to taste
Freshly ground black pepper, to taste

Wash and dry the squid thoroughly. Cut the bodies crosswise into rings 3/4 inch wide and the tentacles into bite-sized pieces. (If the tentacles are small, leave them whole.)

In a large skillet over medium heat, warm 1/4 cup of the olive oil. Add the squid and stir and toss for 5 to 8 minutes, or until tender. Do not overcook or the squid with toughen. Season with salt. Using a slotted spoon, transfer the squid to a large sieve and drain. Set aside to cool.

In a large portable bowl with a lid, combine the cooled squid, the remaining 1/2 cup olive oil, the lemon juice and parsley. Toss well. Season with red pepper flakes and black pepper. Cover and refrigerate until ready to pack in a cooler for transporting. *Serves 4*

Zucchini Marinated with Lemon and Mint

Better than zucchini pickles and faster to make, this lemony-mint refreshment
can be packed as easily in a rucksack as a hamper.

1/4 cup plus 2 tablespoons olive oil
2 pounds small zucchini, trimmed and sliced
crosswise 1/8 inch thick

2 tablespoons fresh lemon juice
Salt and freshly ground black pepper, to taste
2 tablespoons chopped fresh mint

In a large skillet over medium heat, warm the 1/4 cup oil. Add half of the zucchini and sauté until golden on both sides, just a few minutes. Remove with a slotted spoon to paper towels to drain. Repeat with the remaining zucchini slices, adding more oil if necessary.

Place the zucchini in a portable container with a lid and drizzle with the remaining 2 table-spoons olive oil and the lemon juice. Season with salt and pepper, toss to coat and sprinkle the mint over the top. Cover tightly and pack for toting. *Serves 6*

Chili-Spiced Jicama and Carrots

Bites like these fire the appetite along with that first sip of beer or lemonade. This salad is perfect to enjoy anywhere, whether you're stretched out on a blanket at the beach or settled on a log in the park.

4 carrots
1/2 cup fresh lemon juice, or to taste, strained
2 medium jicamas, peeled

1 dried ancho chili pepper
1 dried pequin or pasilla chili pepper

Cut the carrots into thin, narrow sticks about 3 inches long. Place in a portable bowl with a lid and add half of the lemon juice. Toss well. Cut the jicamas into sticks the same size and add to the carrots with the remaining lemon juice. Toss well, cover and refrigerate.

In a small frying pan over medium heat, quickly toast the chilies on all sides until brown and fragrant, making sure they don't burn. Let cool and remove and discard the stems. In a spice grinder or in a mortar grind the chilies to a powder.

Dust the carrots and jicamas with the chili powder. Toss well, cover and pack in a picnic basket. *Serves 8*

Baby Artichoke Salad

A delicacy like this one is for an intimate splendor-on-the-grass occasion when you want to impress. The artichokes are not cooked, so the tiniest, freshest little globes are necessary.

Juice of 2 lemons
36 baby artichokes
2 tablespoons chopped fresh Italian parsley

1/2 cup extra virgin olive oil
Salt and freshly ground black pepper, to taste
3 ounces Parmesan cheese

Fill a large bowl two-thirds full of cold water and add to it the juice of 1 lemon.

Cut the stem from each artichoke flush with the base. Snap off the outer green leaves close to the base. Slice off any spiky tips on the remaining pale inner leaves. As each artichoke is trimmed, place it in the citric water.

Remove the artichokes from the water, one at a time, and using a very sharp knife, cut lengthwise into paper-thin slices. Return the

slices to the water. When all the artichokes are sliced, drain them and pat dry with paper towels.

Place the artichokes in a portable bowl with a lid. Add the remaining lemon juice, the parsley, olive oil, salt and pepper. Mix gently but well. Cover and pack in a cooler. Wrap the cheese separately and add to the cooler.

When ready to serve, using a small knife, shave the Parmesan into thin sheets over the salad. *Serves 6*

Watercress and Redleaf Lettuces with Oranges, Red Onions and Fennel

*In this classic combination from North Africa, bright colors and diverse tangy flavors
pair equally well with salty cold cuts, fried chicken or barbecued fish. The special cutting
of the oranges turns them into glistening half-circle slices free of pith.*

1 large bunch watercress, tough stems removed,
    washed and dried
3 large handfuls redleaf lettuces, washed and dried
4 large navel oranges
1/2 bulb fennel
1 small red onion, very thinly sliced
1/2 cup niçoise or Gaeta olives

Vinaigrette:
6 tablespoons fruity olive oil
4 teaspoons balsamic vinegar
4 teaspoons red wine vinegar
1/2 teaspoon salt
Freshly ground black pepper, to taste

Pack the watercress and lettuces in a plastic bag and refrigerate to chill well before packing in a cooler.

Using a sharp knife, cut off the ends of the oranges. Standing the oranges upright, carefully follow the curve of the fruit and cut away the peel and skin. Cut in half lengthwise and then cut each half into thin slices. Place in a portable bowl with a lid.

Remove the core from the fennel bulb and, using a very sharp knife, shave the bulb thinly with the grain. Add the fennel, onions and olives to the oranges and pack in a cooler for the picnic.

To make the vinaigrette, in a jar with a tight-fitting lid, combine the olive oil, vinegars, salt and pepper. Cover tightly and shake to mix. Pack in the cooler for transporting.

When ready to serve, combine half of the vinaigrette with the orange mixture and half with the greens. Arrange the orange mixture on a single large plate or individual plates. Distribute the greens around or over the arrangement. *Serves 4*

Roasted Garlic

Use this fragrant purée in place of mayonnaise on nearly any picnic sandwich. It is also heavenly brushed on bruschetta.

1 large head garlic
1/4 cup olive oil
1/4 teaspoon salt
Freshly ground black pepper, to taste

Preheat the oven to 325 degrees F.

Cut approximately 1/4 inch off the top of the garlic head. Remove the outer skin but leave the cloves intact. Place the head in a small baking dish and drizzle with the olive oil. Sprinkle with the salt and pepper.

Cover and bake 30 to 45 minutes, or until the garlic is very soft and sweet. When cool enough to handle, squeeze individual cloves onto bread, or squeeze them all into a portable container with a lid and save in the refrigerator for up to 3 days. Pack in cooler for transporting.
Makes approximately 1/4 cup

Clockwise: Olives Spiced with Lemon and Herbs (recipe p. 30), Arugula, Roasted Red Pepper and Prosciutto Panini (recipe p. 43), Roasted Garlic, and Tomato, Red Onion, Mozzarella and Three-Basil Salad

Tomato, Red Onion, Mozzarella and Three-Basil Salad

This legendary Italian combination is the all-time easiest summer salad and a showcase for perfectly vine-ripened tomatoes. Serve it with crusty bread and anything else you want. If you can't find different kinds of basil, using only the sweet green variety is fine.

3 pounds ripe tomatoes (any color), at room temperature, thickly sliced
1 red onion, very thinly sliced
1 cup fresh basil leaves (any combination of sweet green, purple, lemon, cinnamon, or chocolate), coarsely chopped
6 to 8 ounces good-quality fresh mozzarella, thickly sliced
1/4 to 1/3 cup extra virgin olive oil
4 to 6 tablespoons balsamic or red wine vinegar
Salt and freshly ground black pepper, to taste
Sprigs of fresh basil

On a large portable platter, layer the tomatoes, onion slices and basil as you would for lasagna. Top with the mozzarella. Drizzle with the olive oil and sprinkle with the vinegar. Season with salt and pepper and garnish with sprigs of basil.

Cover the platter with plastic wrap and pack in a cooler. *Serves 4*

Olives Spiced with Lemon and Herbs

Even though appetites rarely need stimulating outdoors, pungent tidbits like these olives are always welcome. They are reminiscent of those found in markets in Provence, where you can choose from over a score of varieties of spiced and brined olives. Makes several batches. They need a month in the marinade.

*4 cups unpitted green olives, or a combination of
    niçoise and Moroccan green and black olives,
    drained*
Approximately 1 cup virgin olive oil
2 tablespoons chopped fresh rosemary
1 tablespoon chopped fresh thyme

2 fresh red chili peppers, cut into long, narrow strips
4 large cloves garlic, crushed
6 white peppercorns, crushed
6 black peppercorns, crushed
Zest of 1 lemon, cut into long, narrow strips
1 teaspoon mustard seeds, crushed

Place the olives on a work surface and lightly crush with the back of a heavy knife. This will cause them to absorb more of the flavors.

In a small saute pan, heat 1/2 cup of the olive oil over medium heat. Add all the remaining ingredients except the olives and warm for approximately 3 minutes, or until the herbs and spices release their aromas.

Place the olives in a quart jar or ceramic container. Add the warm oil-herb mixture and then as much of the remaining olive oil as needed to cover the olives. Let cool, then cover and refrigerate for 1 month before serving. They will keep for several months in the refrigerator.

Pack the olives in a leakproof container in a picnic basket. *Makes 4 cups*

Asian Tomato, Broccoli and Buckwheat Noodle Salad

Ease of transport and versatility make this salad ideal as an entree or as a side dish with grilled meats or fish.

2 to 3 cups broccoli florets, lightly steamed and chilled
1/4 cup rice wine vinegar
1/4 cup soy or tamari sauce
2 tablespoons finely chopped fresh ginger
1 teaspoon finely chopped garlic
1/2 cup roughly chopped green onions
1/2 to 1 teaspoon toasted sesame oil, to taste
1/3 cup dry-packed sun-dried tomatoes, soaked in
    warm water to cover for 3 minutes, drained and
    coarsely chopped, or 2/3 cup seeded and
    chopped fresh tomatoes
1/4 teaspoon red pepper flakes (optional)
1/2 pound dried Japanese buckwheat noodles
2 teaspoons toasted sesame seeds

Place the steamed broccoli in a large portable bowl. In a smaller bowl, stir together the vinegar, soy sauce, ginger, garlic, green onions and sesame oil. Pour the mixture over the broccoli and add the tomatoes and the red pepper flakes, if you want a spicy salad.

Bring a large pot of salted water to a boil, add the noodles and cook according to the package directions. Drain and rinse under cold running water to cool completely. Add to the broccoli-tomato mixture and sprinkle with the sesame seeds. Toss gently but thoroughly. Cover and pack in a picnic basket. *Serves 4*

Salad of Herbs

The best time to make this unusual salad with its sweet-tart dressing is in the heat of summer, when herbs are sold in bouquets. Assemble a variety of herbs, including watercress, arugula, cilantro, mint, oregano, Italian parsley, basil and dill, in any combination.

10 cups assorted loosely packed herb sprigs and leaves,
    washed and dried

Lemon Dressing:
1/4 cup olive oil
2 tablespoons Champagne vinegar or
    white wine vinegar
1 tablespoon fresh lemon juice
2 tablespoons minced shallots
1/2 teaspoon salt
1/4 teaspoon freshly ground black pepper
1/2 to 1 teaspoon granulated sugar, or to taste

Place the herbs in a large portable bowl with a lid and refrigerate to chill well before packing in a cooler.

To make the lemon dressing, in a leak-proof container, whisk together the olive oil, vinegar, lemon juice, shallots, salt and pepper. Whisk in enough sugar to balance the flavors. Cover tightly and pack in the cooler.

When ready to serve, toss the herbs with the dressing. *Serves 4*

Fava Beans with Sun-Dried Tomato Oil and Pancetta on Frisée

A link with our earliest relatives, fava beans date back to the Stone Age when all eating was done outdoors. Fresh fava beans, which grow easily in most climates, are divine in this earthy combination, but cooked dried lima beans can be substituted. The oil must be made at least three days in advance of assembling the salad. Use the extra oil in vinaigrettes or to drizzle over bruschetta.

Sun-Dried Tomato Oil:
2 cups extra virgin olive oil
3/4 cup dry-packed sun-dried tomatoes, coarsely chopped

1 pound shelled fresh fava beans (approximately 5 pounds unshelled)
1/2 cup sun-dried tomato oil
2 teaspoons grated lemon zest
Juice of 1 lemon
3 cloves garlic, finely chopped

2 tablespoons finely chopped fresh parsley
1 tablespoon finely chopped fresh oregano
1/4 cup coarsely chopped dry-packed sun-dried tomatoes
Salt and freshly ground black pepper, to taste
1/4 pound pancetta or bacon, thinly sliced and then cut into long, narrow strips
1 head frisée, outer leaves discarded, washed and dried
Shaved Asiago cheese, for garnish

To make the sun-dried tomato oil, heat the olive oil until almost smoking. Place the tomatoes in a heatproof container. Pour the hot oil over the tomatoes and let stand for a minimum of 3 to 4 days. Strain the oil into a bottle, cover tightly and store in a cool, dark place. Put the sun-dried tomatoes in a jar and refrigerate for future use. You will have 2 cups oil; pour off 1/2 cup oil to use in the salad.

If the fava beans are not quite small and tender, boil them in water to cover for approximately 5 minutes, or until the skins begin to pull away from the beans. Drain and peel off the skins. Taste for tenderness. If necessary, boil for 3 to 5 minutes longer, or until the beans are soft but not mushy. Drain again.

In a large portable bowl with a tight-fitting lid, combine the sun-dried tomato oil, lemon zest and juice, garlic, parsley, oregano and sun-dried tomatoes. Add the still-warm beans and toss well. Let stand for approximately 1 hour. Season with salt and pepper.

In a small skillet over medium heat, sauté the pancetta until slightly crisp, just a few minutes. Using a slotted spoon, remove the pancetta from the pan to paper towels to drain. When cool, pack in an airtight container or lay over the beans.

Break the frisée leaves into large bite-sized pieces. Place in a plastic bag and refrigerate until well chilled before packing in a cooler. Pack the shaved cheese in a small container or sprinkle over the top of the beans. Pack the beans (and the pancetta and cheese, if separate) in a cooler.

When ready to serve, arrange the frisée on individual plates or a serving platter. Top with the beans, pancetta and cheese. *Serves 4*

SANDWICHES

There's something for everyone in this chapter, from novice to advanced picnicker. Most of the sandwiches are based on vegetables, and many are designed to be served open-faced, which adds to their visual appeal.

I love the idea of setting out loaves of crusty bakery bread on the picnic table and surrounding them with containers of caponata and garlicky white bean purée for fellow pic-nickers to spread as they like. If a barbecue is handy, the bread can be grilled and brushed with a bit of olive oil to make Italian bruschetta.

I've stretched the definition of sandwiches to include Dolmas Made with Chard Leaves and Prosciutto Stuffed with Red Chard. Flaky phyllo-encased squares of Greek Spinach Pie and a Frittata with Chard and Roasted Red Peppers, with no crust at all, have been slipped in here as well, as they are easily eaten with your hands at any picnic, from breakfast through sunset.

Marinated Tomatoes and Peppers, Roasted Garlic Mayonnaise and Brie Sandwiches

Here, quintessentially satisfying flavors are combined in baguettes for two.
To make these sandwiches for a crowd, quadruple the ingredients and tuck them in a round
sourdough loaf that has been split in half horizontally. Cut it into wedges to serve.

1 medium-sized ripe tomato, seeded and
coarsely chopped
1/2 red or yellow bell pepper, seeded, deribbed and
very thinly sliced
3 tablespoons extra virgin olive oil, plus additional for
roasting garlic
1 tablespoon balsamic vinegar

Salt and freshly ground black pepper, to taste
4 cloves garlic
1/4 cup commercial mayonnaise
2 lengths baguette, each 8 inches long, split in
half horizontally
4 to 6 fresh basil leaves
3 ounces Brie cheese, at room temperature

In a small bowl, stir together the tomato, bell pepper, olive oil and vinegar. Add a pinch of salt and pepper. Set aside to marinate.

To roast the garlic, preheat an oven to 325 degrees F. Coat the peeled cloves with olive oil and wrap in a square of aluminum foil. Bake for approximately 25 minutes, or until the cloves are meltingly soft. In a small bowl, mash the garlic. Add the mayonnaise and stir well.

Open the baguette pieces and place cut side up. Spread the mayonnaise generously on one side of each pair. Place 2 or 3 leaves of basil on top of each mayonnaise-coated half. Spread half of the Brie on each of the other 2 halves. Top the cheese with the marinated tomatoes and peppers. Close up the sandwiches, cut in half if desired and wrap tightly in plastic wrap. Pack in cooler. *Serves 2*

Roasted Chicken and Watercress Sandwiches
with Cranberry Orange Apple Relish

Herb-roasted chicken is jazzed up with a tart fruit relish on these wintertime sandwiches. They would be scrumptious on a mushroom-identifying trek in the forest or on a cross-country skiing outing in the mountains. If you are rushed for time, any sliced roasted chicken or turkey can be used. These sandwiches can also be served open-faced.

Cranberry Orange Apple Relish:
1 pound (4 cups) cranberries
2 Granny Smith apples, unpeeled, cored and coarsely chopped
2 oranges, unpeeled, quartered and coarsely chopped
2 cups granulated sugar

1 roasting chicken (3 to 4 pounds)
Salt and freshly ground black pepper, to taste
1/4 cup olive oil
1 tablespoon slivered lemon zest
Juice of 1 lemon, strained
4 teaspoons fresh thyme or 2 teaspoons crushed dried thyme

2 teaspoons fresh rosemary or 1 teaspoon crushed dried rosemary
1 teaspoon fresh marjoram or 1/2 teaspoon crushed dried marjoram
2 cloves garlic, finely chopped
1 cup water
1/2 cup small green Greek olives (optional)

Commercial mayonnaise, to taste
1 baguette, cut crosswise into 8 equal sections and the sections split horizontally
Unsalted butter, to taste
Watercress sprigs

To make the cranberry orange apple relish, place the cranberries in a food processor and process until finely chopped. Transfer to a medium bowl. Finely chop the apples and then the oranges in the food processor, each time turning the chopped fruit into the bowl with the chopped cranberries. Add the sugar to the fruit and stir well. Refrigerate for several hours. The relish can be frozen or stored in the refrigerator for up to 4 weeks. *Makes approximately 5 cups*

Preheat the oven to 450 degrees F. Rub the exterior of the chicken with salt and pepper. In a small bowl, combine the olive oil, lemon zest and juice, all the herbs, the garlic and a bit more pepper. Brush the chicken generously with the oil mixture, inside and out. Place the chicken on a roasting rack in a roasting pan. Pour the remaining oil mixture over the chicken.

Add the water to the roasting pan. Place in the oven and immediately reduce the heat to 350 degrees F.

Bake for 1 to 1 1/2 hours, basting the chicken with the pan juices every 20 minutes, until the meat is tender. Add the olives to the

roasting pan, if you wish, during the last 30 minutes of cooking. Remove from the oven and let cool.

To prepare the sandwiches, spread some mayonnaise on one cut side of each baguette section, and some butter on the other cut side. Pull off the meat from the roasted chicken, place on the buttered bread and top with peppery sprigs of watercress and some of the relish. Wrap the sandwiches in plastic wrap and put the olives in a small, tightly covered container for serving on the side. Pack the sandwiches and olives in the picnic basket in winter, in the cooler on a hot day. *Serves 8*

Left to right: Arugula, Roasted Red Pepper and Prosciutto Panini and
Garlicky White Bean Purée with Broccoli di Rape (recipe p. 44)

Arugula, Roasted Red Pepper and Prosciutto Panini

*Tart arugula, sweet red peppers and salty prosciutto combined on focaccia or French rolls bring
a taste of Italy to a lakeside or rowing picnic for four. If the peppers are full flavored, you can make
the prosciutto optional or substitute herbed goat cheese for the prosciutto and the mayonnaise.
Another alternative is to grill the peppers and the eggplant at the picnic site.*

2 large red bell peppers
4 slices eggplant, each approximately 1/4 inch thick
Olive oil
Salt, to taste
1/2 cup commercial mayonnaise
1 1/2 teaspoons fresh lemon juice
1 small clove garlic, mashed in a mortar or minced

1/4 cup fresh basil leaves, cut into fine ribbons
12 ounces focaccia, quartered and split horizontally,
    or 4 soft French rolls, split horizontally
4 thin slices prosciutto (approximately 2 ounces)
1 large bunch arugula, tough stems removed, washed
    and dried
Freshly ground black pepper, to taste

Preheat the oven to 400 degrees F. To roast the peppers, place them on a baking sheet in the oven for 30 minutes, turning several times. The skins should appear loose and be slightly charred. Remove from the oven and, when just cool, slip off the skins, cut in half and remove the stems, seeds and ribs.

To bake the eggplant, brush both sides of each slice with olive oil, sprinkle with salt and place on a baking sheet. Bake in the oven, turning once, for approximately 30 minutes, or until soft when pierced. Set aside.

In a small bowl, stir together the mayonnaise, lemon juice, garlic and basil. Salt to taste.

To make the sandwiches spread the mayonnaise liberally on the split bread. Then layer on the prosciutto, arugula and roasted pepper and sprinkle with salt and pepper to taste. Top with the eggplant slices. Wrap the sandwiches in plastic wrap and pack in a cooler. *Serves 4*

Garlicky White Bean Purée with Broccoli di Rape

Not only for vegetarian picnickers, this nutritious combination belongs in every sandwich maker's repertoire.
The sprinkling of chili in the broccoli di rape topping adds a little fire to each bite.

White Bean Purée:
1 cup dried cannellini or other white beans
3 cups water
2 tablespoons light olive oil
1 bay leaf
4 cloves garlic
1 sprig fresh thyme
1 teaspoon salt
1 tablespoon peppery extra virgin olive oil

Broccoli di Rape Mixture:
1 large bunch broccoli di rape
2 tablespoons light olive oil
1/2 teaspoon salt
1/8 teaspoon red pepper flakes (optional)

Bruschetta (recipe p. 57), baguette slices or crackers

To make the white bean purée, soak the beans in cold water to cover by 2 inches for 8 hours or overnight. Drain and place in a saucepan with the 3 cups water, the light olive oil, bay leaf, garlic and thyme. Bring to a boil and reduce the heat to medium-low. Simmer, uncovered, for 45 minutes, then add the salt. Simmer for an additional 15 minutes, or until the beans are tender and the liquid is almost absorbed.

Remove from the heat. Take out the bay leaf and thyme sprig and discard. Stir in the peppery olive oil. Pass the beans and their liquid through a food mill placed over a large bowl or purée in a blender or food processor. Place in a portable container with a lid and store in the refrigerator until it is time to pack in a cooler for the picnic.

To make the broccoli mixture, cut off the coarse stems of the broccoli di rape and discard. Finely chop the remaining stems, leaves, and flower heads into 1/4-inch pieces. In a large pan over medium heat, warm the olive oil and add the broccoli. Sprinkle with the salt and red pepper flakes (if using) and sauté for approximately 10 minutes, or until tender but not mushy. Let cool and adjust the seasonings. Transfer to a portable bowl with a lid and refrigerate until it is time to pack in a cooler for transporting.

To serve, liberally spread the bean purée on the bread. Top with a spoonful of the broccoli di rape mixture. Alternatively, set out bowls of the bean purée (drizzled with extra olive oil, if desired), broccoli and bread and let the picnickers help themselves. *Serves 4 to 8*

Open-Faced Watercress Sandwiches

*Expanding the horizon of picnic sandwiches to dainties like these adds an element of surprise
and elegance. Put on your wide-brimmed hat and summer whites, invite friends to a picnic tea next
to your favorite babbling brook and lay out these sandwiches along with others from this chapter.*

1 large bunch watercress, tough stems removed,
    washed and dried
30 pesticide-free nasturtium flowers
1/2 pound cream cheese (preferably without
    additives), at room temperature

1/4 cup finely chopped yellow onion
1/2 cup peeled, seeded and finely chopped cucumber
1/2 teaspoon salt
1/8 teaspoon freshly ground black pepper
8 slices fine-grained country white, wheat or egg bread

Set aside a handful of the watercress leaves for garnish. Finely chop the rest, which should yield a good 1/2 cup. Wash and dry the nasturtium flowers, checking carefully for bugs that like to hide inside. Select 8 flowers for garnish, pack them in a plastic bag, blow in air and tie securely. Refrigerate, then pack in a cooler. Cut the remaining flowers into long, narrow strips.

In a medium portable bowl with a lid, stir together the cream cheese, onion, cucumber, chopped watercress, flowers, salt, and pepper until well blended. Let the flavors meld for at least 1 hour. Pack in the cooler. Pack the bread in a picnic basket.

When ready to serve, spread the cheese mixture on the bread slices and garnish with the reserved watercress leaves and a confetti of the whole nasturtium petals. These sandwiches are lovely open-faced, but they can also be closed with a second piece of bread and wrapped in plastic wrap or paper before packing them for the picnic. *Serves 2 to 4*

Prosciutto Stuffed with Red Chard

*Using creative license, you can stretch the sandwich
point with these little appetizer roll-ups. Tender chard
makes a garlicky counterpoint to the salt-cured prosciutto—
perfect for a midsummer patio picnic.*

1 bunch red Swiss chard, tough stems removed, washed and dried
2 tablespoons light olive oil
2 cloves garlic, finely chopped
1/2 teaspoon salt
1 tablespoon red wine vinegar
2 tablespoons extra virgin olive oil
16 very thin slices prosciutto (1/3 to 1/2 pound)

Stack the chard leaves and slice them lengthwise into
thin ribbons. Then roughly chop them crosswise.

In a large sauté pan over medium heat, warm the
olive oil. Add the greens, garlic and salt and sauté until
the greens are tender, 7 to 10 minutes. Stir in the vinegar
and remove from the heat. Add the extra virgin olive
oil and let rest until just cool enough to handle.

Place a tablespoonful of the warm filling on the
short edge of each piece of prosciutto and roll up. If
desired, cut the rolls in half. Wrap the rolls in aluminum
foil or place in a portable container and pack in a picnic
basket. *Serves 4 to 8*

*Left to right: Open-Faced Watercress Sandwiches (recipe p. 45)
and Prosciutto Stuffed with Red Chard*

Frittata with Chard and Roasted Red Peppers

A natural for, but not limited to, a breakfast picnic, this colorful egg pie can be made the night before.
It also makes a protein-rich appetizer or main course anytime. Some frittatas basically consist of beaten eggs and
vegetables, rather like a baked omelet. In this recipe, bread crumbs add stability and cheese adds richness.

1 bunch Swiss chard, stalks removed, washed and dried
1 large leek, chopped (approximately 1 cup)
2 tablespoons unsalted butter
1 tablespoon olive oil
1 teaspoon minced fresh thyme
1 teaspoon minced fresh marjoram
1 teaspoon salt, plus salt to taste

2 large red bell peppers, roasted and coarsely chopped
6 eggs
1/2 cup milk
1/2 cup fresh bread crumbs
1/2 cup grated fontina cheese
1/2 cup grated Parmesan cheese
Freshly ground black pepper, to taste

Preheat the oven to 350 degrees F. Butter a 9-inch square baking dish.

Stack the chard leaves and cut crosswise into ribbons. In a large pan over medium heat, sauté the leeks in the butter and oil for approximately 5 minutes, or until soft. Add the chard, thyme, marjoram and the 1 teaspoon salt and sauté for approximately 7 minutes, or until the chard is tender. Remove from the heat, stir in the peppers and let cool.

In a large bowl, beat the eggs with the milk until blended. Add the bread crumbs and cheeses and then stir in the chard mixture. Season to taste with salt and pepper. Transfer to the prepared baking dish.

Bake the frittata for approximately 40 minutes, or until the center is firm and the crust is golden. Remove from the oven and let cool. Transfer to a portable serving dish and wrap well in plastic wrap. Pack in a cooler and cut into squares for serving. *Serves 4 to 6*

Greek Spinach Pie

*Once again, the sandwich idea is stretched, but these squares of phyllo-wrapped spinach
are irresistible, especially when you are coordinating a Mediterranean or Greek theme picnic.*

1/2 pound phyllo pastry (usually available in
    1-pound packages)
1 1/2 pounds spinach (1 very large bunch or
    2 small to medium ones), stems removed,
    washed and dried
1/2 yellow onion, finely chopped
2 green onions, finely chopped
1 tablespoon light olive oil
1/4 cup chopped fresh dill or 2 teaspoons dried dill
2 tablespoons chopped fresh mint (10 to 12 leaves)

1/2 teaspoon ground cumin, preferably
    freshly ground
Pinch of nutmeg, preferably freshly grated
2 eggs
1/4 pound feta cheese, crumbled
1/4 pound cottage cheese
2 ounces grated kasseri or Romano cheese
    (approximately 1/2 cup)
1/4 teaspoon freshly ground black pepper
6 tablespoons unsalted butter, melted

If the phyllo is frozen, thaw it overnight in the refrigerator. Remove the phyllo from the wrapping, lay out the stack of sheets and, if you have purchased a 1-pound package, cut them in half widthwise. Cover the portion you will be using with plastic wrap and a damp kitchen towel. Tightly wrap the remaining sheets in plastic wrap and return to the refrigerator where they will keep well for at least a week.

    Finely chop the spinach leaves. In a large pan over medium heat, sauté the yellow onion and green onions in olive oil for 5 minutes, or until softened. Add the spinach, dill, mint, cumin and nutmeg and stir until the spinach is soft and the liquid has evaporated. Let cool.

In a large bowl, beat the eggs lightly. Add the feta, cottage and kasseri cheeses, the spinach mixture, and the pepper. Mix well.

    Preheat the oven to 375 degrees F. Brush a 9-by-13-inch rectangular baking dish with a little of the melted butter. Place a sheet of phyllo in the bottom of the dish, letting the edges of the sheet come up the sides of the dish, and brush with a little of the melted butter. Repeat until you have used up half of the sheets, lightly brushing each one with butter. Spread the filling evenly on top. Fold the edges of the phyllo dough over the filling. Continue layering the remaining sheets of phyllo, again brushing each layer with butter. Brush the top

Left to right: Greek Spinach Pie and Dolmas Made with Chard Leaves (recipe p. 52)

layer with butter. Brush the top layer with melted butter as well. Tuck the edges down along the insides of the dish. Score the top of the pie into squares or diamonds with a knife. Be careful not to slice through the bottom layer or all the juices will leak into the pan.

Bake for approximately 1 hour, or until the pie is crisp and golden brown. Remove from the oven, let cool completely and finish cutting the squares or diamonds through. Top with aluminum foil and pack in the cooler. Serve from the baking dish. Alternatively, pack in a single layer in a portable container. *Serves 6 to 10*

Dolmas Made with Chard Leaves

Call these leaf sandwiches or reverse sandwiches. Typically made with grape leaves,
this version substitutes chard and calls for braising the dolmas in the oven to meld the flavors.

1/4 cup pine nuts
1 bunch Swiss chard (approximately 20 leaves),
    washed
1 yellow onion, finely chopped
3 tablespoons light olive oil
1 cup long-grain white rice
1/2 cup finely chopped fresh parsley

1/2 cup chopped fresh dill or 4 teaspoons dried dill
1/2 cup dried currants
1 1/4 teaspoons salt
4 teaspoons fresh lemon juice
1 cinnamon stick
5 cups water, boiling
1 lemon, cut into wedges

Preheat the oven to 350 degrees F. Place the pine nuts in a shallow pan and toast them for approximately 5 minutes, or until golden and fragrant. Remove and let cool. Leave the oven set at 350 degrees F.

Remove the tough stalks from the chard leaves. With a sharp knife, cut out the tough section of the central rib that protrudes into the leaf, being careful not to cut the leaf in half. Bring a large pot of salted water to a boil, add the chard leaves and blanch for 30 seconds. Drain and refresh immediately in cold water, then drain again. Carefully spread out the leaves on paper towels to absorb extra moisture.

In a medium-sized saucepan over medium heat, sauté the onion in 2 tablespoons of the olive oil for 7 to 10 minutes, or until soft. Add the rice, parsley, dill, currants, 3/4 teaspoon of the salt, 2 teaspoons of the lemon juice and the cinnamon stick. Add 2 cups of the boiling water, cover and simmer for approximately 15 minutes, or until the water is absorbed. Let the mixture cool to room temperature and remove the cinnamon stick.

Spread half of the remaining 1 tablespoon of olive oil in a 10-inch round or 9-inch square glass baking dish. Lay one of the chard leaves on a plate with the raised veins facing up. If the leaf has a tear in the center, overlap the edges so that there is no hole. Place a heaping tablespoonful of the rice mixture at the base end of the leaf and roll up, tucking in the sides as you roll. Place the dolma, seam side down, in the dish. Continue with the remaining leaves and rice mixture. The dolmas should be tightly packed into the pan. Rub the remaining oil on top of the dolmas.

Combine 1 cup of the boiling water with the remaining 2 teaspoons lemon juice and 1/2 teaspoon of the salt. Pour over the dolmas. Place

a second baking dish of the same size on top of the dolmas to act as a weight. Pour the remaining 2 cups boiling water into the top dish.

Bake the dolmas in the oven for 30 minutes until bubbling and the leaves are very tender. Remove from the oven and let cool. Holding both dishes together, carefully pour off the water in both dishes. Arrange the dolmas in a portable container with a lid. Wrap the lemon wedges in a plastic bag or a portable container. Pack both containers in a picnic basket. *Makes approximately 20 pieces; serves 4 to 8*

GRILLED MORSELS

For many lovers of the outdoors, a picnic without a barbecue is like a romance without a mate. Unless a smoky halo lingers in our hair, what's the point of carting all that food somewhere? Whether on a Weber in the backyard, on a grill at the park or over a pit fire at the beach, cooking over coals brings out our primal natures. It harkens us back to simpler times. We want to watch that raw morsel cook before our eyes.

A lively selection of items for the grill follows. For a midsummer dinner, cook the whole meal on the grill. Barbecued Salmon with Strawberry, Mint and Cucumber Salsa, Rosemary Potato Skewers and Grilled Polenta with Sun-Dried Tomato Pesto make a delicious trio for an Independence Day menu. For a simpler celebration, lay a slice of eggplant or chicken hot off the grill between slices of crusty baguette.

Top to bottom: Caponata on Bruschetta (recipe p. 57) and Greek Islands Sea Bass (recipe p. 56)

Greek Islands Sea Bass

This simple grilled fish, topped with Greek feta cheese and olives and fresh tomatoes, is a Mediterranean centerpiece. Accompany this dish with Dolmas Made with Chard Leaves (recipe p. 52) and Greek Spinach Pie (recipe p. 50) for an extraordinary twilight event that should be set overlooking vineyards or the sea.

Herb-Infused Oil:
1/2 cup virgin olive oil
3 sprigs of fresh oregano, finely chopped
2 teaspoons grated lemon zest
3 cloves garlic, finely chopped

1 pound ripe tomatoes, seeded and coarsely chopped
2/3 cup Kalamata or other high-quality brine-cured olives, pitted
4 to 6 ounces feta cheese
1 lemon, cut into wedges
2 pounds fresh sea bass, swordfish or other meaty fish, cut into 4 steaks

To make the herb-infused oil, in a saucepan over medium heat, warm the olive oil for 1 minute. Remove from the heat and add the oregano, lemon zest and garlic. Allow the oil to sit at room temperature for at least 1 hour or, for best results, overnight. Store in a portable leakproof container.

Pack the tomatoes, olives, feta cheese and lemon wedges in separate portable containers. Cut the fish into 4 equal portions, wrap well and pack in a portable container with a lid. Refrigerate until ready to leave for the picnic, then place everything in a cooler.

At the picnic site, toss the tomatoes with half of the herb-infused oil. Crumble the feta.

Prepare a charcoal fire, preferably with mesquite. When the coals are ready, brush the fish with some of the infused olive oil and place them in a well-oiled fish-grilling rack. (A grilling rack is not necessary, but it simplifies the cooking and turning of the fish.)

Place the rack over coals about 4 inches from the fire and grill 3 to 4 minutes on each side, turning once and brushing with the infused oil again after turning. (The general rule for cooking fish is that it will take approximately 10 minutes total cooking time for each inch of thickness. Measure the thickest part of the fish fillets to determine the cooking time.)

Place fish on individual plates. Garnish with a few generous tablespoons of the tomatoes, olives and feta. Drizzle the remaining infused olive oil over each fillet and serve the lemon wedges on the side. *Serves 4*

Caponata on Bruschetta

Italy's sweet-sour vegetable melange is at home on slices of the grilled bread brushed with olive oil known as bruschetta. You can make the caponata up to a week in advance. Assemble the sandwiches just before eating.

Caponata:
1 medium-sized eggplant, sliced 1/2 inch thick
Salt
1 medium-sized yellow onion
2 small celery stalks
1 small red bell pepper, seeded and deribbed
1/4 cup extra virgin olive oil
1/2 cup red wine vinegar
2 tablespoons light brown sugar
1 tablespoon finely chopped garlic
2 tablespoons pine nuts

2 or 3 medium-sized tomatoes, seeded, chopped and
    excess juices squeezed out
1/2 cup brine-cured black olives, drained, pitted and
    coarsely chopped
1/4 cup loosely packed fresh basil leaves, finely chopped
3 tablespoons capers, drained
2 to 3 tablespoons raisins, chopped

Bruschetta:
8 slices baguette or Italian bread, each approximately
    1 inch thick
Approximately 2 tablespoons extra virgin olive oil
1 tablespoon finely chopped garlic

To make the caponata, place the eggplant slices on paper towels, sprinkle with salt and let stand for 15 minutes to drain off excess moisture. Pat the eggplant slices dry.

Chop the eggplant, onion, celery and bell pepper into approximately 1/2-inch pieces. In a heavy sauté pan over medium heat, warm the oil. Add the vegetables and sauté for approximately 10 minutes, or until soft. Add the vinegar, sugar and garlic and simmer for 5 minutes longer.

Meanwhile, in a small, heavy sauté pan over medium heat, stir and toss the pine nuts until they brown lightly. Let cool.

Transfer the vegetables to a medium bowl

and let cool to room temperature. Add the tomatoes, pine nuts, olives, basil, capers and raisins. Stir well, place in a portable container with a lid and pack in a picnic basket.

Wrap the bread in plastic wrap or place in a plastic bag. Combine the olive oil and garlic in a small leakproof portable container. Pack everything, including a basting brush, in the picnic basket.

At the site, prepare a charcoal fire and let the coals burn down. Using the brush, lightly but completely coat both sides of each bread slice with the garlic oil. Grill on both sides, turning once, until lightly toasted. Generously mound some caponata on top of each slice. *Serves 4*

Grilled Polenta with Sun-Dried Tomato Pesto

*Italian and proud of it, polenta gets an American accent when
placed on the barbecue at your favorite picnic site.*

Polenta:

6 cups water
1 teaspoon salt
2 cups polenta
1/2 cup (1 stick) unsalted butter, cut into pieces
1 tablespoon chopped fresh rosemary,
*   basil or oregano*
1/2 cup grated Italian grana cheese (such as
*   Parmesan, Asiago or pecorino)*

Sun-Dried Tomato Pesto:

1/4 cup toasted pine nuts or slivered almonds
1 cup dry-packed sun-dried tomatoes
Warm water or heated dry red wine,
*   to cover tomatoes*
2 or 3 cloves garlic
1/4 cup grated Italian grana cheese
4 or 5 fresh basil leaves
3/4 to 1 cup extra virgin olive oil
1 teaspoon salt
Juice of 1/2 lemon
Pinch of red pepper flakes (optional)

In a heavy-bottomed, 3-quart saucepan, bring the water to a boil. Add the salt and gradually stir in the polenta. Reduce the heat to low and stir frequently for 15 to 30 minutes, or until the polenta thickens. It should become thick and creamy. The more you cook the polenta, the smoother it becomes. Stir in the butter, rosemary and cheese. Pour the warm polenta into a lightly oiled rimmed baking sheet or shallow roasting pan. Cover and refrigerate until thoroughly chilled.

To prepare the sun-dried tomato pesto, preheat the oven to 350 degrees F. Place the pine nuts or almonds in a shallow pan and toast them for approximately 5 minutes, or until golden and fragrant. Let cool.

Meanwhile, in a bowl, soak the sun-dried tomatoes in warm water or red wine to cover for approximately 10 minutes, or until plump. Drain off the liquid.

In a blender or food processor, combine the sun-dried tomatoes, toasted nuts and garlic and process until smooth. Add the cheese and basil and process until mixed. With the motor running, gradually add the olive oil, adding just enough to form a smooth sauce the texture

of thick mayonnaise. Season with salt, lemon juice and red pepper flakes (if using). Pack 1 cup of the pesto in a leakproof portable container. (The leftover pesto can be refrigerated for up to two weeks.)

Remove the chilled polenta and cut into squares. Place in a portable container in a single layer and pack with the pesto in a picnic basket.

Prepare a charcoal fire, preferably with mesquite or other hardwood coals. When the coals are ready, brush the polenta with olive oil and place on the grill rack. Grill, turning once, until browned on each side and heated through. (Plan on 2 to 3 minutes on each side.) To serve, spoon the pesto on top of or alongside the polenta squares. *Serves 6 to 8*

Grilled Eggplant, Tomatoes, Provolone and Pesto Sandwiches

Grilled eggplant has an uncanny meaty consistency that is enhanced by the tomato,
cheese and garlicky basil flavors in this filling sandwich. Bring Country French Potato Salad
(recipe p. 20) and a bottle of Chianti to round out the meal.

4 large slices eggplant, each 1/2 inch thick
Salt, to taste
Extra virgin olive oil
1 baguette

1/4 cup basil pesto, homemade or commercial
4 slices tomato, each 1/2 inch thick
4 slices provolone cheese (approximately 3 ounces total)
2 small handfuls arugula

Place the eggplant slices on paper towels in a portable container. Sprinkle with salt and drizzle with olive oil and cover tightly. Separately pack the baguette, pesto, tomato, cheese and arugula, and then pack everything but the cheese in a picnic basket. Pack the cheese in the cooler.

Prepare the charcoal fire. Pat the eggplant slices dry with the paper towels. When the coals are ready, grill the eggplant slices, turning once, until browned and softened. This will take only a few minutes on each side.

To make the sandwiches, split the baguette in half horizontally and then cut in half crosswise. Spread the pesto on both cut sides of each piece. Cover one side with tomato slices and provolone. Cover the other side with eggplant and top with arugula. Close up the sandwiches, slice in half and serve. Alternatively, make the sandwiches at home, wrap well and pack in a basket for the picnic. *Serves 2*

Rosemary Potato Skewers

Potato enthusiasts and anyone else who takes a bite will be hooked on the smoky herbaceousness emanating from these hot potato wedges. For the best results, use firm red, Yellow Finn or White Rose potatoes. For an extra infusion of rosemary, tie several sprigs of the herb together to make a basting brush or throw a couple of sprigs on the coals just before putting the skewers on the grill.

4 medium potatoes (approximately 1 1/3 pounds),
    peeled and cut into 1 1/2-inch chunks
1 tablespoon olive oil
1 tablespoon salted butter or margarine, melted
1 tablespoon chopped fresh rosemary, or 1 teaspoon
    dried rosemary

1 large clove garlic, minced
1/2 teaspoon salt
1/4 teaspoon freshly ground black pepper

Four 12-inch metal skewers or 4 bamboo skewers
    soaked in warm water for 30 minutes, drained

In a heavy saucepan with a tight-fitting lid, cook the potatoes in 2 inches of salted boiling water for 15 minutes, or until the potatoes are tender. Drain, let cool slightly and then thread onto the metal or bamboo skewers. Pack in a portable container and place in a picnic basket.

In a portable leakproof bowl, stir together all the remaining ingredients. Pack in a picnic basket.

Prepare a charcoal fire. When the coals are ready, place the potato skewers on the grill 3 to 4 inches above the glowing embers. Brush the skewers with the rosemary mixture. Grill, basting and turning several times, for 10 to 12 minutes, or until lightly browned. *Serves 4*

Grilled Chicken Sandwich with Red Pepper Mayonnaise

Here, succulent citrus-marinated chicken breasts are grilled, spiced with hot-pepper mayonnaise and accompanied with sweet tomatoes, bitter frisée and tangy artichoke hearts on split sourdough sandwich rolls. These meals-on-a-roll can also be wrapped and packed for a day hike to enjoy during a trailside picnic.

Lemon Marinade:
1 tablespoon chopped fresh rosemary
1 teaspoon chopped fresh thyme
1 tablespoon red pepper flakes (optional)
3 bay leaves, crushed
4 cloves garlic, chopped
5 strips orange zest, diced
5 strips lemon zest, diced
2 tablespoons fresh lemon juice
1 cup extra virgin olive oil

6 large chicken breasts, boned, skinned, and
*   excess fat removed*

Red Pepper Mayonnaise:
1/2 yellow sweet bell pepper
3 hot red cherry peppers or 1 tablespoon red pepper flakes
3 large cloves garlic, peeled
1 cup commercial mayonnaise

Sandwich:
1 small head frisée, washed and dried
36 red cherry tomatoes, stems removed, then cut in half
12 marinated artichoke hearts, sliced lengthwise
Salt and freshly ground black pepper, to taste
Chopped fresh flat-leaf parsley, to taste
6 sourdough sandwich rolls or 2 sourdough baguettes,
*   divided into thirds*

To make the marinade, in a small bowl, combine all the ingredients and mix well. Set aside.

Place the chicken breasts between 2 pieces of waxed paper and, using a meat mallet, flatten lightly. Place the chicken in a portable container with a leakproof lid. Pour in the marinade, turn to coat the chicken, cover and refrigerate for 2 hours or for up to overnight. Pack in the cooler to take to the picnic.

To make the red pepper mayonnaise, char the bell pepper and cherry peppers (if using) over an open gas flame or charcoal grill or in the broiler until blackened and blistered. When cool enough to handle, peel off the blackened skin and seed and derib. In a food processor or blender, combine the bell pepper, cherry peppers and garlic. Pulse until puréed. Fold the red pepper purée into the mayonnaise. Place in a portable container with a lid and refrigerate until ready to pack in the cooler.

Pack the frisée in a plastic bag and refrigerate to chill well. In a small portable bowl with a lid, combine the cherry tomatoes and artichokes. Season with salt, pepper and parsley and toss well. Pack both the greens and the vegetables in the cooler.

Prepare the charcoal fire. When the coals are ready, remove the chicken from the marinade and pat dry. Discard the marinade. Brush the grill rack with a little oil. Grill the breasts over a medium-hot fire until lightly charred and golden, approximately 5 minutes on each side. Set aside and keep warm.

Split the rolls in half horizontally and toast on the cut sides over the coals. Coat the cut sides with some of the red pepper mayonnaise. Place some frisée and a chicken breast on the bottom half of each roll. Top with the other half of the roll and serve with the tomato-artichoke mixture on the side. *Serves 6*

Barbecued Salmon with Strawberry, Mint and Cucumber Salsa

Every Fourth of July, the world's largest salmon barbecue takes place in Noyo Harbor in northern California, attracting some five thousand people. See the All-American Independence Day Barbecue menu on page 13 for accompaniments for your own summer celebration.

Strawberry, Mint and Cucumber Salsa:
1 English (seedless) cucumber, finely chopped
1 green onion, thinly sliced
1 tablespoon fresh mint leaves, cut into thin strips
3 to 4 tablespoons seasoned rice wine vinegar
2 cups fresh strawberries, hulled and finely diced

Barbecue Sauce:
1/2 cup (1 stick) unsalted butter
1 clove garlic, finely chopped
1 tablespoon honey
2 tablespoons soy sauce
1 tablespoon fresh lemon juice

6 skinless salmon fillets, approximately 6 ounces each

For the best results, prepare the salsa shortly before leaving for the picnic. In a medium portable bowl, mix together the cucumber, green onion, mint and vinegar. Cover with plastic wrap and refrigerate for 1 hour. Pack the strawberries in a separate portable container and refrigerate. Place both containers in a cooler.

To prepare the barbecue sauce, in a small saucepan over low heat, melt the butter with the garlic. Stir in the honey, soy sauce and lemon juice and cook for 2 minutes. Set aside. Let cool slightly and pack in a portable leak-proof container. Be sure to pack a basting brush and, if you have one, a fish-grilling rack. Pack the salmon in a portable container, cover tightly and refrigerate to chill well before packing in the cooler.

Prepare a fire in a charcoal grill. When the coals are ready, brush the sauce on both sides of the salmon fillets and place them in a well-oiled fish-grilling rack. (A grilling rack is not necessary, but it simplifies the cooking and turning of the fish.)

Place the rack over coals about 4 inches from the fire and grill 4 to 5 minutes on each side, turning once and brushing with the sauce again after turning. (The general rule for cooking fish is that it will take approximately 10 minutes total cooking time for each inch of thickness. Measure the thickest part of the fish fillets to determine the cooking time.) Baste the fish again with barbecue sauce as it finishes cooking. The fish is done when it is just barely firm and resistant to the touch.

To serve, open the rack and remove the fish fillets with a spatula. Transfer to a platter. Stir the strawberries into the cucumber mixture and serve on top of the salmon. *Serves 6*

SWEETS

Picnics always activate my sweet tooth. Fruit-rich and sugary, pies, tarts and cakes that I could otherwise resist hold all the intrigue of an illicit liaison when I'm outdoors. Feeling reckless in the fresh air, I can't wait until the tart is cut, the cake uncovered, the berries spooned over the shortcake. It's true everything tastes better outside, but desserts are the best.

Here is something sweet for every occasion. Contemporary renditions of old-fashioned picnic standards include a Black, Golden and Red Raspberry Tart, an American Apple Pie, an Apple and Dried Cranberry Crisp and a unique Tomato Ginger Upside-Down Cake. Tart Lemon Squares and a Strawberry Grapefruit Mint Compote are also offered as post-barbecue restoratives. And Blueberry Banana Muffins double as trail snacks and sunrise breakfast treats.

Marionberry Peach Crunch

If marionberries are not in your neighborhood, substitute olallieberries, loganberries, boysenberries, blackberries or raspberries. Take this in early summer for a breakfast picnic or for dessert. It can be baked in a heavy glass dish or, for lighter transport, in a reusable aluminum foil baking pan.

Crunch Topping:
1 cup steel-cut rolled oats
1 cup all-purpose flour
1/2 teaspoon ground cinnamon
1/2 cup firmly packed dark brown sugar
1/2 cup (1 stick) margarine or unsalted butter, cut into small pieces
1 cup chopped pecans (optional)

Fruit Filling:
Approximately 1 pound peaches, peeled, pitted and cut into slices 1/2 inch thick (3 cups)
3 cups marionberries
3/4 cup granulated sugar
2 tablespoons all-purpose flour

Preheat the oven to 350 degrees F.

To make the crunch topping, in a medium bowl, combine the oats, flour, cinnamon and brown sugar. Add the margarine or butter and, using your fingertips, work it in until the mixture is crumbly. Add the pecans, if desired, stir well and set aside.

To make the filling, in a medium bowl, toss together the peaches and berries. Add the sugar and flour and stir gently to coat the fruit well.

Spoon the filling into a 6-by-9-inch glass baking dish (or aluminum pan). Spread the topping evenly over the fruit.

Bake for 1 hour, or until the top is golden brown and the fruit is bubbling. Let cool slightly before packing, then top with aluminum foil or invert an aluminum foil baking pan on top and secure with kitchen string or rubber bands. Carry in the picnic basket. *Serves 6*

Strawberry Grapefruit Mint Compote

*Tart and sweet combine in this palate-refreshing treat. Serve it
after fried chicken or barbecued ribs, on a breakfast picnic or at poolside.*

1 large grapefruit
1 cup strawberries, hulled and halved

2 teaspoons granulated sugar
1 teaspoon roughly chopped fresh mint leaves

Cut the top and bottom off the grapefruit. Using a sharp knife, cut away all the peel and pith from the outside of the grapefruit. Then, angling the knife to cut toward the center of the fruit, follow the section lines to produce delicate segments without any skin or pith.

In a medium portable bowl, gently mix the grapefruit segments, strawberries, sugar and mint. Cover and refrigerate until ready to pack into a picnic basket or cooler. *Serves 4*

Blueberry Banana Muffins

*Two popular fruits fill these moist muffins. Carry the muffins in a basket for a breakfast picnic,
pack them on top of your backpack for the first day on the trail, or tote them to a garden for a picnic tea.*

1/2 cup (1 stick) margarine, at room temperature
3/4 cup granulated sugar
2 eggs
2 to 3 bananas, mashed (approximately 1 cup)
1/2 cup milk

2 cups all-purpose flour
2 teaspoons baking powder
1/2 teaspoon ground cinnamon
2 cups fresh or frozen blueberries

Preheat the oven to 375 degrees F. Grease 12 muffin-tin cups or line with paper liners.

In a medium bowl with an electric mixer, beat together the margarine and sugar until light and fluffy. Add the eggs, one at a time, beating well after each addition. Mix in the bananas and milk.

In a large mixing bowl, combine the flour, baking powder and cinnamon. Add the margarine mixture to the dry ingredients and mix only until the batter is moist.

Carefully stir in the whole blueberries. If you are using frozen blueberries, add them while they are still frozen or they will turn the batter purple. Spoon the batter into the prepared muffin tin, filling the cups to the top. Bake in the oven for 30 to 35 minutes, or until muffins are golden brown.

Let cool for 5 minutes in the muffin pan, then transfer to a cooling rack. The muffins can be stored in a tightly sealed plastic container or in plastic bags in the refrigerator for up to 4 days.
Makes 1 dozen muffins

Prizewinning Orange Scones with Berries and Cream

Light and flaky, these scones double as a breakfast bread and the base for shortcake.
Make these once and you won't be able to dine on your picnic blanket again without them.
For the shortcakes, use all strawberries or a combination of seasonal berries.

Scones:
2 cups sifted all-purpose flour
1 tablespoon baking powder
1 teaspoon salt
2 tablespoons granulated sugar
5 1/2 tablespoons unsalted butter, cut into pieces
1 extra-large egg
1/2 cup whipping cream
2 tablespoons unsalted butter, melted

1/2 cup granulated sugar
1 tablespoon grated orange zest

6 to 8 cups fresh berries (such as strawberries,
*   raspberries, blackberries and tayberries), hulled*
*   (if necessary), washed and well dried*
3/4 to 1 cup granulated sugar, depending upon
*   sweetness of berries*
1 to 1 1/2 cups whipping cream, whipped and lightly
*   sweetened with 2 teaspoons granulated sugar*

Preheat the oven to 425 degrees F. Lightly grease a baking sheet.

To make the scones, in a small bowl, stir together the flour, baking powder, salt and sugar. Using a pastry blender or 2 knives, cut in the butter until the mixture is the consistency of coarse meal. In a small bowl, lightly beat the egg and then stir in the cream. Add to the flour mixture and stir just until blended.

Turn out the dough onto a lightly floured board and knead for 1 minute. Roll out into a rectangle approximately 4 inches by 8 inches. Brush with the melted butter. Sprinkle with the sugar and orange zest. Starting from a long side, roll up, jelly-roll fashion, and seal the seam by pinching it together lightly with your fingers.

Cut the roll crosswise into 8 slices, each 1 inch thick. Lay the slices cut side down on the prepared baking sheet. Bake for 12 to 15 minutes, or until golden. Let cool on a rack and pack into plastic bags. Place in a picnic basket.

Slice the strawberries and leave the other berries whole. Place all the berries in a large portable bowl. Sprinkle with the sugar, cover and refrigerate for 1 to 2 hours, then pack in a basket or cooler to carry to the picnic. Put the whipped cream in a leakproof container and refrigerate until well chilled before packing in the cooler. To serve, heap spoonfuls of berries over a scone and top with whipped cream.
Serves 8

*Left to right: Prizewinning Orange Scones with Berries and Cream
and Blueberry Banana Muffins (recipe p. 73)*

Black, Golden and Red Raspberry Tart

This is the perfect picnic tart. Cornmeal in the crust ensures a crisp base and the rich cheese filling a sublime taste. To pack the tart, place an inverted aluminum pie pan over the top and secure it with kitchen string or rubber bands. Keep it in a cool place until ready to serve.

Venetian Cornmeal Crust:
3/4 cup all-purpose flour
1/2 cup fine yellow cornmeal
1/4 teaspoon salt
1/2 teaspoon baking powder
1/4 cup (1/2 stick) unsalted butter, at room temperature
6 tablespoons granulated sugar
1/4 teaspoon vanilla extract
1/2 tablespoon grated lemon zest

1 egg yolk
1 to 2 tablespoons dark rum or water

Filling:
4 ounces cream cheese, at room temperature
1/4 cup whipping cream
1/3 cup plus 1 tablespoon confectioners' sugar
1/4 teaspoon vanilla extract
4 ounces mascarpone cheese
2 cups assorted raspberries (a combination of black, golden and red), washed and well dried

Preheat the oven to 350 degrees F.

To make the crust, in a medium bowl, combine the flour, cornmeal, salt and baking powder. In a food processor, combine the butter and granulated sugar. Process until light and fluffy. Add the vanilla, lemon zest, egg yolk and enough rum or water to hold dough together. Pulse until blended.

Transfer the mixture to the bowl containing the dry ingredients. Stir until well mixed. The dough should be sticky and thick. Gather into a rough ball and wrap in waxed paper. Refrigerate for 30 to 60 minutes.

Knead the dough 4 or 5 times on a lightly floured surface. Sprinkle a little flour on the dough and the rolling pin to prevent sticking, then roll out the dough into a round about 10 inches in diameter and about 1/4 inch thick. If the dough is too sticky to roll easily, roll out between 2 sheets of waxed paper.

Drape the dough round over the rolling pin and carefully transfer it to a 9-inch tart pan with a removable bottom. Lightly press the dough into the pan. If it tears, simply press the edges together again. Trim the overhang even with the rim.

Line the dough with aluminum foil and fill with 2 cups of pie weights or uncooked rice or beans. Bake for 20 minutes. Remove the pie weights and foil and bake for an additional 12 minutes, or until the crust browns slightly. Remove from the oven. Let cool for 5 minutes. Carefully remove the outside ring of the pan. Using a long metal spatula, gently slip the tart shell off the metal bottom onto a cooling rack. Let cool for 30 minutes.

Place the cooled tart shell on a serving plate and cover with plastic wrap until ready to fill.

To make the filling, in a large bowl, place the cream cheese, whipping cream, confectioners' sugar and vanilla. Using an electric mixer, beat until fluffy. Then, using a flexible spatula, fold in the mascarpone.

Spread the filling in the cooled tart crust with the flexible spatula. Top with the black, golden and red raspberries, arranging the berries in concentric· circles. Cover and refrigerate for 30 minutes or as long as overnight. Pack for transporting as described in the headnote and slip into a cooler. *Serves 6 to 8*

Apple and Dried Cranberry Crisp

An autumn classic, this rendition of apple crisp is nutty and piquant.
Because the cranberries are dried and any kind of apple can be used, it can be made year-round.
When the ice-cream maker is going, a scoop of homemade vanilla on the side is heavenly.

Topping:
1/2 cup pecan halves
1 cup all-purpose flour
1/3 cup firmly packed light brown sugar
1/4 cup granulated sugar
1/8 teaspoon ground cinnamon
1 tablespoon grated orange zest
1/3 cup unsalted butter, at room temperature

Filling:
6 apples (such as Golden Delicious or Idared),
*   approximately 2 pounds, quartered, cored,*
*   peeled and sliced*
1 tablespoon granulated sugar, or to taste
1/2 cup dried cranberries

Preheat the oven to 350 degrees F.

To make the topping, spread the pecans on a baking pan and toast for approximately 5 minutes, or until lightly browned and fragrant. Let cool and chop. Set aside. Raise the oven temperature to 375 degrees F.

In a large bowl, stir together the flour, brown and granulated sugars, cinnamon and orange zest. Add the butter and, using your fingertips, work it in until the mixture resembles coarse sand. Mix in the pecans and set aside.

To make the filling, place the apples in a bowl and sprinkle with the sugar. Add the dried cranberries and stir to mix. Place the filling in a 8- or 9-inch square or round baking dish, level the surface and then spoon the topping evenly over the top.

Cover with aluminum foil and bake for 20 minutes. Remove the foil and continue baking for 20 minutes, or until the top is crisp and browned and the apples are tender. Pack in a portable container with a lid in a picnic basket.
Serves 6 to 8

American Apple Pie

*America's quintessential picnic pie also loves a bit of cheese. Save a piece of Cheddar
from your sandwich makings to serve with this delectable pie. After all, "apple pie without cheese
is like a kiss without a squeeze." For a simpler presentation, top with a plain crust.*

Crust:
3 cups all-purpose flour
1 teaspoon salt
1 cup chilled shortening, lard, margarine or
    unsalted butter, cut into bits
1/3 cup milk
1 egg
2 tablespoons unsalted butter, melted

Filling:
2 1/2 pounds sweet-tart firm apples, cored,
    quartered, peeled and sliced (8 cups)
1 tablespoon granulated sugar
2 tablespoons all-purpose flour
1 teaspoon vanilla extract
1/2 cup half-and-half

To make the crust, in the bowl of a mixer fitted with the paddle attachment, sift together the flour and salt. Add the shortening and beat on low speed until the mixture is the consistency of fine cornmeal.

In a small bowl, whisk together the milk and the egg and pour into the flour mixture. Increase the speed to medium and beat until the dough forms a ball and pulls away from the sides of the bowl. Divide the dough into 3 equal portions, flatten into disks and wrap separately in plastic wrap. Refrigerate 2 portions for at least 20 minutes or for up to 1 day. To save for another use, refrigerate the other portion for 1 day or freeze for up to 1 month.

Preheat the oven to 425 degrees F. Select a 9- or 10-inch pie plate.

On a heavily floured surface, roll out 1 dough portion into a round 1/8 inch thick and approximately 2 inches larger in diameter than your pie plate. Drape the dough round over the rolling pin and carefully transfer it to the pie plate. Press in gently and trim the dough so that it hangs approximately 1/2 inch over the edge. Fold the overhang under and press against the rim. Brush the bottom and sides of the crust with the melted butter and set aside.

To make the filling, in a large bowl, toss together the apples, sugar and flour. Add the vanilla and half-and-half and mix well. Spoon the filling into the prepared crust.

To make the lattice top, roll out the second dough portion into a round of about the same size and thickness as the bottom round. Using

a sharp knife, cut it into strips 1/2 to 3/4 inch wide. Pick up the two longest strips (at the center of the round) and cross them over the center of the filled pie crust. Then lay half of the strips about 3/4 inch apart across the pie. Now, fold back every other strip from the center and place a cross strip close to the center of the pie. Unfold the folded strips. Repeat in this manner, working from the center of the pie to the rim, until half of the pie is covered in a woven pattern. Repeat on the other half of the pie. Trim the ends of the strips even with

the edge of the bottom crust. Lift the ends of the strips and brush the edges of the bottom crust with water. Press the strips gently but firmly against the rim and then softly flute the edges.

Bake for 10 minutes. Reduce the temperature to 350 degrees F. and bake 30 to 40 minutes, or until the crust is golden and the apples are tender.when pierced with a thin knife blade. Let cool completely on a rack. Invert an aluminum pie plate over the top and secure in place with rubber bands or string. (Or cover with aluminum foil.) Pack in a picnic basket. *Serves 8 to 10*

Tomato Ginger Upside-Down Cake

This comes from an eighteenth-century cookbook, when tomatoes were more available than pineapple.
The spicy cake and ginger-tomato topping make an easily packable conversation-piece dessert for any picnic.

1/2 cup (1 stick) unsalted butter, melted, plus 1/2 cup
    (1 stick) unsalted butter, at room temperature
1 tablespoon grated fresh ginger
6 tablespoons plus 1 1/2 cups firmly packed light
    brown sugar
2 or 3 ripe tomatoes (or enough to cover the bottom of
    the pan as you would for a pineapple upside-down
    cake), peeled, seeded and sliced 1/4 inch thick

1/2 cup molasses
2 1/2 cups unbleached all-purpose flour
2 teaspoons baking powder
1 tablespoon ground ginger
1/2 teaspoon ground cloves
1 cup buttermilk

Preheat the oven to 350 degrees F.

In a bowl stir together the melted butter, grated ginger and the 6 tablespoons brown sugar. Spread evenly on the bottom of a 10-by-14-inch baking pan. Cover with the tomato slices.

In a medium bowl, combine the room-temperature butter, the 1 1/2 cups brown sugar and the molasses. Using an electric mixer, beat until light and creamy. In another bowl, sift together the flour, baking powder, ground ginger and cloves. Add the flour mixture alter-nately with the buttermilk to the butter mixture. Pour the batter over the tomatoes in the baking pan.

Bake for approximately 40 minutes, or until a toothpick comes out clean when inserted in the center. Remove from the oven, run a knife around the sides of the cake to loosen it and then invert onto a platter larger than the baking pan. Let stand at least 5 minutes before trying to lift off the pan. Let cool and wrap in plastic before packing in the picnic basket. *Serves 6 or more*

Lemon Squares

These tart addictive bites are refreshing after a wealth of picnic fare.
Be sure to keep them in a cool place until ready to eat. (photo p. 84)

Crust:
3 1/2 cups all-purpose flour
1/4 cup confectioners' sugar
1/4 teaspoon salt
3/4 pound plus 4 tablespoons (3 1/2 sticks)
    unsalted butter, cut into small pieces

Filling:
6 large eggs
3 cups granulated sugar
1 tablespoon grated lemon zest
1/2 cup strained fresh lemon juice
2/3 cup all-purpose flour
1 teaspoon baking powder
Confectioners' sugar, for dusting

Preheat the oven to 350 degrees F. To make the crust, in a large bowl, sift together the flour, sugar and salt. Using a pastry blender or 2 knives, cut the butter into the mixture until it is the consistency of coarse cornmeal. Gather the dough into a rough ball and, using your fingertips, press it onto the bottom and up the sides of a 17-by-12-by-1-inch baking sheet. Bake for 15 minutes, or until lightly browned. Remove from the oven and leave the oven set at 350 degrees F.

To make the filling, in a large bowl, beat the eggs well and then beat in the sugar. Add the zest and stir in the lemon juice. Sift the flour and baking powder together into the egg mixture and beat until smooth. Pour the mixture evenly into the baked crust.

Bake for 25 minutes, or until set. Let cool completely in the pan on a rack. Using a sharp knife, carefully cut into squares and dust with confectioners' sugar. Pack in a single layer in a portable container and take to the picnic in a cooler. *Makes 4 dozen squares*

BEVERAGES

Thirst is a given when you are outside, and seasoned picnickers automatically reach for the customary wine, beer and soft drinks. A jug of water is always welcome, and backpackers often tote water filters and flavored thirst-quenching powders. But, like sandwich and salad combinations, beverages come in a wide variety.

The following recipes contain a number of intriguing suggestions to perk up the old repertoire. They range from a tart lemonade and a sweet Strawberry Pineapple Smoothie to a lemon-zapped beer and a fresh tomato juice–based Bloody Mary with an optional alcoholic hit. The Blackberry Spritzer is another delightful fruity concoction, while a sprightly Sparkling Cider Punch is enhanced by a shot of potent applejack.

Bray's Lemonade

When it's hot, no other flavor quenches thirst like lemon. In this creation, sweetened lemon juice is frozen into ice cubes. Pack the cubes in a thermos and add chilled soda water just before serving.

Simple Syrup:
2 cups granulated sugar
4 cups cold water

3 cups lemon juice (approximately 12 large lemons), strained
3 cups cold water
3 cups soda water or ice water
Sprigs of fresh mint

To make the simple syrup, combine the sugar and the 4 cups water in a saucepan and bring to a boil over high heat, stirring with a wooden spoon until the sugar dissolves. Continue to boil for 5 minutes, without stirring, and then remove from the heat. Let cool, then refrigerate in a covered container. (It will keep for 3 to 4 weeks.)

In a large pitcher, combine 1 cup of the simple syrup, 1 1/2 cups of the lemon juice and the 3 cups water. Stir well, pour into ice cube trays and freeze.

To pack for the picnic, combine the remaining 1 1/2 cups lemon juice, the remaining simple syrup and the ice cubes in a thermos and pack in a cooler. Put the soda water and the mint sprigs (in a portable container) in the cooler.

When ready to serve, stir together the 3 cups soda water and the contents of the thermos, mixing well. Pour into tall glasses. Garnish each serving with a mint sprig and hand out straws. *Makes 6 drinks*

Blackberry Spritzer

Any favorite berries can be substituted here to make a lively fruit base for drinks.
If ice is unavailable, make this with chilled soda water.

Blackberry Syrup:
8 cups fresh or frozen blackberries
1 cup granulated sugar, or to taste

3 cups soda water
Ice cubes
Lemon twists, for garnish (optional)

To make the blackberry syrup, place the black–berries in a food processor and pulse until partly puréed. In a saucepan, heat the berry purée to a boil, then simmer for about 5 minutes until the juice is released. Place a sieve over a bowl and pour in the berry purée. Gently press the juice through the sieve with the back of a wooden spoon until only the seeds remain.

Return the berry juice to the saucepan. Add the sugar and bring to a boil, stirring until the sugar is dissolved. Remove from the heat and let cool, then pour into a portable leak-proof container and refrigerate. (You will have approximately 3 cups syrup. It can be stored in the refrigerator for up to 1 month.)

Pack the syrup, soda and ice cubes sepa-rately in a cooler. If using the lemon twists, place in a plastic bag and pack in the cooler as well.

To make the spritzers, fill 6 tall glasses with ice cubes. Pour 1/2 cup blackberry syrup into each glass. Fill the glasses with soda water and top with a lemon twist, if desired. *Makes 6 drinks*

Strawberry Pineapple Smoothie

Fruit smoothies are fresh and filling—perfect for the outdoors. Blend this just before leaving for your picnic, and be sure to shake before serving.

1/2 cup fresh pineapple chunks
1 cup fresh or frozen strawberries, hulled (if necessary) and halved or sliced
1 banana, sliced into 1/2-inch pieces
2 cups buttermilk
1 to 2 tablespoons honey
3 or 4 fresh mint leaves
4 ice cubes
4 fresh strawberries or pineapple chunks, for garnish

Place all the ingredients except the garnish in a blender and purée until smooth. Pour into a chilled thermos and pack in a cooler or picnic basket. Pack the fruit garnish in a portable container and tuck into the cooler or basket.

To serve, shake the thermos, then divide the smoothie among 4 tall glasses. Garnish each drink with fruit cut three-fourths of the way through and perched on the lip of the glass. *Serves 4*

Lemon Shandy

Here are two versions of an old English sailors' libation. The lemon cuts the bitterness and lightens up the beer, making it a popular summer refreshment.

Version I:
Juice of 1 lemon
2 cups soda water, chilled
6 cups ale or lager (four 12-ounce bottles), chilled

Put the lemon juice in a leakproof container and pack in a cooler. Pack the soda and ale or lager separately in the cooler.

When ready to serve, for each drink, combine one-fourth of the lemon juice and 1/2 cup of the soda water in a 14-ounce mug or insulated cup. Slowly pour 1 1/2 cups (1 bottle) of the ale or lager into each mug or cup and serve. *Makes 4 drinks*

Version II:
1 cup lemonade
6 cups beer (four 12-ounce bottles), chilled

Pour the lemonade into a thermos and refrigerate to chill well. Pack the lemonade and beer separately in a cooler.

When ready to serve, for each drink, pour 1/4 cup of the lemonade into a 14-ounce mug or insulated cup. Slowly pour 1 1/2 cups (1 bottle) of the beer into each mug or cup and serve. *Makes 4 drinks*

Bloody Mary

The fresh tomato juice in this version of a Bloody Mary is so outstanding, you may want to skip the vodka.
If tomatoes aren't at their peak, canned juice can be substituted. Don't reserve these cool drinks strictly for breakfast.
The spicy tartness makes a marvelous refreshment for hot- or cold-weather picnics anytime of the day.

Approximately 6 pounds (2 quarts) very ripe, juicy
    tomatoes or 4 cups canned tomato juice
Salt, sugar and fresh lemon juice for seasoning tomato
    juice, if needed
1/4 cup finely chopped red onion
1 fresh red or green jalapeño chili pepper, finely chopped
4 tablespoons finely chopped cucumber (optional)
Juice of 2 limes
1 to 2 tablespoons Worcestershire sauce

Salt, to taste
Freshly ground black pepper, to taste
6 jiggers vodka
Tabasco sauce, to taste
4 celery stalks, for garnish
1 lime, cut into quarters, for garnish
4 jumbo shrimp, peeled, deveined, cooked and
    chilled, for garnish (optional)
Crushed ice cubes

To prepare the tomato juice from fresh tomatoes, chop the tomatoes coarsely. Place them in a stainless-steel pot and bring to a simmer over low heat. Cook until the tomatoes soften completely and their juices are released. Remove from heat and let cool. To remove the seeds and skin, run the tomatoes and juice through a food mill, fine sieve or juicer placed over a bowl. Let stand for approximately 30 minutes. Tomatoes that contain significant amounts of water may separate, causing the water to rise to the top. If this happens, skim off the water. If necessary, keep skimming as long as the juice keeps separating. The more water you remove, the thicker the tomato juice.

Taste the juice. Remember, this is not canned. It might taste slightly bland without the salt, sugar and citric acid used by commercial canners to bring out the flavors. It should have a heavy, rich tomato aroma. If the flavor doesn't quite meet your specifications, add salt, sugar and/or lemon juice to suit your palate. Refrigerate the juice immediately. It will keep for a few days, but the flavor diminishes with time.

Pour the tomato juice into a 2-quart thermos. Add all the remaining ingredients except the celery, lime quarters, shrimp (if using) and ice cubes . Mix well and pack in a cooler. Pack the garnishes and ice cubes separately.

To serve, fill 4 tall glasses with ice and divide the tomato juice mixture among them. Garnish each glass with a celery stalk and lime quarter. If you are in a particularly flamboyant mood, top each drink with a jumbo shrimp.
Makes 4 drinks

Hot Rum and Cider

*Whether carried by you or your Saint Bernard, this is the perfect toddy for a cool northern
California summer picnic as well as for a winter trailside reprieve. I always make it after a day of
pressing apples, when the end of the harvest is celebrated with a nighttime barbecue.*

2 tablespoons unsalted butter, at room temperature
1 1/2 tablespoons maple sugar
2 whole cloves
2 long orange zest strips

1 cinnamon stick
1/2 cup dark rum
3 cups apple cider, heated

In a small bowl, beat together the butter and sugar until smooth and creamy. Set aside.

Stud 1 clove in each orange zest strip. In a preheated 1-quart thermos, place the zest, cinnamon stick and rum. Pour in hot cider and top with the butter mixture. Cap tightly and pack in a picnic basket or backpack.

To serve, pour into mugs. *Serves 4*

Sparkling Cider Punch

Slightly sweet and bubbly, this drink is spiked with applejack, a brandy distilled from apple cider. Serve it postpicnic, when everyone is ready to play a game of cards by the light of the Coleman lantern.

4 teaspoons superfine sugar
2 teaspoons fresh lemon juice
1/2 cup applejack

12 ice cubes (optional)
Sparkling cider

Pack the sugar in a portable container in a picnic basket. Put the lemon juice and applejack in separate leakproof containers and pack in a cooler along with the ice cubes (if using) and the sparkling cider.

To serve, put 1 teaspoon sugar, 1/2 teaspoon lemon juice and 2 tablespoons applejack in each of 4 tall glasses. Add 3 ice cubes to each glass, if you have them. Then fill each glass to the top with sparkling cider. *Makes 4 drinks*

INDEX

METRIC CONVERSIONS

Liquid Weights

U.S. Measurements	Metric Equivalents
1/4 teaspoon	1.23 ml
1/2 teaspoon	2.5 ml
3/4 teaspoon	3.7 ml
1 teaspoon	5 ml
1 dessertspoon	10 ml
1 tablespoon (3 teaspoons)	15 ml
2 tablespoons (1 ounce)	30 ml
1/4 cup	60 ml
1/3 cup	80 ml
1/2 cup	120 ml
2/3 cup	160 ml
3/4 cup	180 ml
1 cup (8 ounces)	240 ml
2 cups (1 pint)	480 ml
3 cups	720 ml
4 cups (1 quart)	1 litre
4 quarts (1 gallon)	3 3/4 litres

Dry Weights

U.S. Measurements	Metric Equivalents
1/4 ounce	7 grams
1/3 ounce	10 grams
1/2 ounce	14 grams
1 ounce	28 grams
1 1/2 ounces	42 grams
1 3/4 ounces	50 grams
2 ounces	57 grams
3 1/2 ounces	100 grams
4 ounces (1/4 pound)	114 grams
6 ounces	170 grams
8 ounces (1/2 pound)	227 grams
9 ounces	250 grams
16 ounces (1 pound)	464 grams

Temperatures

Fahrenheit	Celsius (Centigrade)
32°F (water freezes)	0°C
200°F	95°C
212°F (water boils)	100°C
250°F	120°C
275°F	135°C
300°F (slow oven)	150°C
325°F	160°C
350°F (moderate oven)	175°C
375°F	190°C
400°F (hot oven)	205°C
425°F	220°C
450°F (very hot oven)	230°C
475°F	245°C
500°F (extremely hot oven)	260°C

Length

U.S. Measurements	Metric Equivalents
1/8 inch	3 mm
1/4 inch	6 mm
3/8 inch	1 cm
1/2 inch	1.2 cm
3/4 inch	2 cm
1 inch	2.5 cm
1 1/4 inches	3.1 cm
1 1/2 inches	3.7 cm
2 inches	5 cm
3 inches	7.5 cm
4 inches	10 cm

Approximate Equivalents

1 kilo is slightly more than 2 pounds
1 litre is slightly more than 1 quart
1 centimeter is approximately 3/8 inch